THE **NEXT** RESURRECTION

YOU MAY NEVER DIE!

Hilton Sutton, Th.D.

HSM Publications
Roman Forest, Texas

THE NEXT RESURRECTION

The Next Resurrection by Hilton Sutton Th.D.

Unless otherwise noted, all Scripture quotations are from the New King James version of the Bible. Copyright © 1979, 1980, 1982 by Thomas Nelson, Inc., publishers.

Cover Design: Kristin Miller

ISBN 1-879503-23-9
Library of Congress catalog card number: 2002106249

Printed in the United States of America

FOREWORD

Carved into the stone archway that forms the entrance to a rural Central American cemetery are the words, "Aqui esperamos la Resurrection"—Here we await the Resurrection." But on that wonderful day when many of those graves are indeed opened, another dramatic event will take place; an event that will forever change the lives of everyone on this planet.

INTRODUCTION

Not since Jesus uttered those famous words recorded in the Gospel of John, Chapter 11, verse 25, "I Am the Resurrection and the Life. He who believes in Me, though he <u>may</u> die, he shall live," have we been so close to the day of that prophesied event. But please notice that Jesus said, "though he MAY die," in the very next verse (26) He tells us, "and whoever lives and believes in Me shall <u>never</u> die".

Jesus clearly connects the moment of <u>The Next Resurrection</u> to a time when many shall never die. If you would like to be one of the many who will never see death, this book is for you.

History records the stories of only two unique individuals, born thousands of years ago, who never died. In fact, they were taken bodily and alive directly to Heaven, or raptured. The following is their story, a story destined to be repeated soon in the lives of many. Will you be one of them?

Contents

ONE

ENOCH: THE FIRST RAPTURE

The first mention of a rapture in the Bible, found in the fifth chapter of the Book of Genesis, involves a man named Enoch. Let's examine what these Scriptures say about him.

> **And Enoch lived sixty and five years, and begat Methusaleh: and Enoch walked with God after he begat Methuselah three hundred years, and begat sons and daughters:**
> **And all the days of Enoch were three hundred sixty and five years: and Enoch walked with God: and he was not; for God took Him.**
>
> **Genesis 5:21-24**

These verses state, *God took him.* He walked with God for 365 years, and he did not die. Notice this event occurred before the flood.

Look now at the eleventh chapter of Hebrews. This chapter is often regarded as God's Hall of Fame of men and women of faith (and it is), but I do not believe it is complete. I am convinced that God's Hall of Fame of men and women of faith is still open and more are being added. (*Your* name may be up for consideration for inclusion in that hall, or it may be already written there!)

In Hebrews 11:5-6 we read:

By faith Enoch was translated that he should not see death; and was not found, because God had translated him: for before his translation he had this testimony, that he pleased God. But without faith it is impossible to please him (God): **for he that cometh to God must believe that he is, and that he is a rewarder of them that diligently seek him.**

By this we know that Enoch was taken *bodily* from the earth to heaven. He did not die, but was translated—received up unto the Lord physically alive. What would you call that, if not a rapture? There is no other way to interpret this verse, no way to explain it away without doing irreparable damage to the Scriptures. On the authority of both the Old and New Testaments, we can safely conclude: *Enoch walked with God: and he was not, for God raptured him.*

The Bible says Enoch was raptured because he walked with God all the years of his life and pleased Him. Enoch pleased God with his faith!

The Measure of Faith

Since Enoch was raptured because he walked with and pleased God by faith, what is to keep believers today from having the same experience? Enoch was not born again or baptized with the Holy Spirit, yet God took him because of his consistent faith. Enoch learned the importance of walking with God from his Great, Great, Great, Great, Great Grandfather, Adam. Adam was still alive when Enoch was born.

There is no such thing as a born-again child of God who does not have faith. Romans 12:3 tells us, **"God hath dealt to every man the measure of faith."** God gives *His* kind of faith —the *God-kind* of faith—the only kind He has.

We know the God-kind of faith is perfect and cannot be improved upon. There can't be anything wrong with God's kind of faith. And Romans 12:3 says God has given it to everyone.

You may ask, "How much is **the** *measure* of faith?" More than enough!

It is impossible for some to receive less than others. God deals to *every* man the measure of faith. Each receives the same amount.

Some teachers state that certain ones receive more faith than others because "they need it." Not true. All of us receive the same amount of the God-kind of faith. When we first hear the Word of God, faith is activated. The first thing it produces for us is the born-again experience. We accept Jesus Christ and are saved by faith (Eph. 2:8).

You may say, "But sometimes I feel like I don't have enough faith, and other times I feel like I don't have any faith at all." That is because you are depending upon your feelings instead of the Word of God. God says you have faith, so you do!

"Then there must be something wrong with my faith," you say. That is not the problem either. God has given you **the** *measure of faith;* that is more than enough. The problem lies with you: either you are not using the faith you have or you are using it improperly.

Let me give you an illustration. You buy a brand-new car. It is parked in your driveway, in perfect running order, full of gasoline, and read to go. But instead of driving it, you walk. A car will do you no good unless you use it.

Sometimes we may not use our faith at all. At other times, we may use it improperly. (You can get into your car, but unless you operate it correctly, it will not perform for you as it was designed.) That does not mean we lack faith or that our faith is inferior. The problem lies in our application of the faith we already have.

Romans 10:17 says, **"So then faith cometh by hearing, and hearing by the word of God."** The Word begins to work within us to activate our believing. Hearing and receiving the Word causes the God-given faith to become active within us. When faith is thus activated, it will produce; and its first product is salvation through the Holy Spirit. A person cannot be saved (born again) without it. God takes advantage of our hearing His Word and conveys His faith into our spirit man (Eph. 2:8).

We can learn to use our faith properly by studying God's Word (which is our textbook), and by putting into action what we learn.

Enoch was able to please God by faith. Because of that, he was raptured to Heaven—the first instance of a rapture in the Scriptures. Even those who claim there is no rapture taught in the Scriptures will agree with this one. We cannot build a doctrine on just this one passage of Scripture, but if we can find more than one reference to a rapture, we can. This was a true experience for Enoch. Let's look further to find out who else had a similar experience.

Two

Elijah: The Second Rapture

The second rapture in the Bible was that of Elijah, the great prophet of God.

James describes Elijah as **a man subject to like passions as we are** (James 5:17). This means he was as human as you and I. As an example, let's look at an incident in 1 Kings 18.

Before his experience of being translated (caught up, snatched away, or raptured), Elijah was walking down a country road one day when the king's chariot pulled up. King Ahab leaned out, looked at Elijah, and said, "You're the man who is bringing all this trouble on Israel."

The prophet of God, a human being just like the rest of us, looked King Ahab in the eye and said boldly, "No King, it is you! You have forsaken the Lord and have followed Baal. I want you and Jezebel—that ungodly, wicked woman you are living with—to gather up all the prophets of Baal and meet me tomorrow on Mount Carmel. We'll have a contest and see whose god is God!"

The Test

They all met on Mount Carmel. There were 450 prophets of Baal, tens of thousands of Israelites, and Elijah. Elijah had already decided he was the only one in all of Israel who had remained true to God. Of course, that was not so.

There, on Mount Carmel, they prepared an altar. Elijah said, "You offer a sacrifice to your god; then I'll sacrifice to mine. The god who answers by fire and consumes the sacrifice is the god all of us will serve."

The prophets of Baal prayed, chanted, and cried to their god until late afternoon. They worked themselves into such a frenzy that they actually cut themselves trying to get their god to act.

Elijah mocked them, "You've had a good time today attempting to get your god to do something, but perhaps he is away on a trip. Let me see what my God will do."

He built a fresh altar, dug a trench around it, put wood on it, and placed a bullock on the wood. Then he had twelve barrels of water poured on the sacrifice until the trench around the altar was filled. When the time came to offer the sacrifice, Elijah stepped back and prayed a short prayer. Then fire from God fell from heaven, consumed the sacrifice, the wood, the stones, and licked up the water out of the ditch! The Israelites fell on their faces before God and repented. Then they took the prophets of Baal into the grove, and Elijah slew them.

King Ahab jumped into his chariot and raced home at full speed. I can hear the brakes screech as he ground to a halt in front of the palace. He leaped out and bounded up the steps, where he met Queen Jezebel.

She took one look at Ahab's ashen white face and asked, "What's the matter? What happened?" Breathlessly, he told her the whole story. Ahab was white, but Jezebel turned fiery red! She sent a messenger to Elijah and said, "As you have done to my prophets and priests, so will I do to you by this time tomorrow!" (1 Kings 19:2).

What do you suppose Elijah did at the threat of this evil, ungodly woman? Elijah—the great prophet of God for whom God had just performed such mighty acts—took off running! Elijah was quite a runner, having once outrun the horses of Ahab's chariot. He ran until he dropped from exhaustion under the shade of a little tree.

As he lay there, he said, **"O Lord, take away my life; for I am not better than my fathers"** (1 Kings 19:4). In other words, "Go ahead and kill me, God. If You don't, Jezebel will!"

After he slept for a while, an angel woke him with a hot plate lunch from heaven's cafeteria. Then Elijah went on his way, refreshed.

Jezebel did not succeed in her threats. God saw to it that Elijah was victorious. Jezebel and Ahab were destroyed, just as Elijah had foretold.

There is a lesson in this for us today: never let the threats of the devil determine your lifestyle, set your mental attitude, or affect your relationship with God. The devil is a deceiver. He loves to lie and he usually does it with threats. If you allow him to get by with it, he will use threats to destroy your effectiveness for God.

As time passed, God spoke to Elijah about a young man named Elisha, who was to succeed him as prophet of Israel. They worked together until the time came for Elijah to pass his prophet's mantle on to Elisha. We read this account in 2 Kings 2:1, 8-11:

> **And it came to pass, when the Lord would take up Elijah into heaven by a whirlwind, that Elijah went with Elisha from Gilgal. And Elijah took his mantle, and wrapped it together, and smote the waters, and they were divided hither and thither, so that they two went over on dry ground.**

And it came to pass, when they were gone over, that Elijah said unto Elisha, Ask what I shall do for thee, before *I be taken away from thee.* And Elisha said, 'I pray thee, let a double portion of thy spirit be upon me.'

And he said, 'Thou hast asked a hard thing: nevertheless, if thou see me *when I am taken from thee*, it shall be so unto thee; but if not, it shall not be so.'

And it came to pass, as they still went on, and talked, that, behold, there appeared a chariot of fire, and horses of fire, and parted them both asunder; and Elijah went up by a whirlwind into heaven.

Anyone who believes the Bible will have to accept that God translated both Enoch and Elijah, bodily and alive, from earth to heaven. In other words, they were raptured. This is the second of the seven biblical raptures.

The person who is the subject of our next chapter is without a doubt the most well-known man in all of history. His life and teachings are both legendary and controversial. Much of the world builds their calendar around His birth.

But unlike Enoch and Elijah, before being raptured, He first passed through Death's door, and back again. His was the first Resurrection. He then ascended bodily and alive to Heaven, in the sight of many witnesses, some forty days later. Of course His name is...

THREE

JESUS: THE THIRD RAPTURE

The record of the third rapture is found in Acts, Chapter 1. On the Sabbath, Jesus and His disciples left the city of Jerusalem and went out to the Mount of Olives. Paul tells us there was a company of more than five hundred who went out with Him (1 Cor. 15:6). There Jesus conveyed His last great message to them. (Read the final chapters of Matthew, Mark, Luke, and chapter 1 of Acts.)

> **And when he had spoken these things, while they beheld, he was taken up; and a cloud received him out of their sight.**
>
> **And while they looked steadfastly toward heaven as he went up, behold, two men stood by them in white apparel; which also said, 'Ye men of Galilee, why stand ye gazing up into heaven? This same Jesus which is taken up from you into heaven, shall so come in like manner as ye have seen him go into heaven.'**
>
> **Acts 1:9-11**

Again, this is a passage of Scripture that no one, even those who do not believe in the Rapture, can discount.

Jesus was taken up alive, bodily. He had been resurrected for forty days. During that time, He had walked on earth, been with His disciples on several occasions, cooked for them, and even eaten with them the same foods He had eaten before His crucifixion.

He seemed to be very natural, yet He had supernatural abilities—He was in his earthly glorified body! When He appeared to His disciples in a closed room, He did not open the door, but passed through the wall (John 20:25-28). He had the unique ability to appear and disappear at will. Mark 16:19; Luke 24:50, 51; along with Acts 1:9-11 clearly establish that Jesus was caught up alive from earth to heaven in His glorified body.

He was in His glorified body at the time of His ascension. However, nothing in the Scriptures indicates that Enoch and Elijah were in glorified bodies when they were taken up. Since Jesus is our example, the Church at its rapture will be in a glorified state, as was Jesus (1 Cor.15: 50-53; 1 John 3:1-3).

Ephesians 5:27 says the Lord will present unto Himself **"a glorious church, not having spot, or wrinkle, or any such thing; but that it should be holy and without blemish."** I do not teach that we will receive glorification before the Rapture. We will, however, be like Him *when we see Him* (1 John 3:2). The instant Jesus appears with a shout, we, by the energies of the Holy Spirit, will overcome the natural law of gravity and, in that same instant, become glorified, departing earth for heaven.

Three biblical accounts of raptures should be enough evidence to establish for anyone the reality of raptures. If God has already raptured two of His saints, and His own Son, why should we not believe He will also rapture us? We are clearly told in the Scriptures that He is going to catch away the Church. Our rapture—the rapture of the Church—is Rapture Number Four.

The Second Coming of Jesus is sometimes mentioned in jest, but to His many followers throughout the centuries since His days here on Earth, it is an event of joyous expectation. It is in fact the second most commonly mentioned theme in all the New Testament.

Only hours before His crucifixion, Jesus Himself told His disciples about His soon departure to Heaven, and His eventual return. We find this story recorded in the Gospel of John, Chapter 14, beginning with verse one. In a calm and reassuring tone, Jesus comforted His disciples saying, "Let not your heart be troubled; you believe in God, believe also in Me. In My Father's house are many mansions; if it were not so I would have told you. I go to prepare a place for you. And if I go and prepare a place for you, <u>I will come again</u> and receive you to Myself, that where I am, there you may be also" (vs 1-3 NKJV).

In only three verses, one short paragraph, Jesus said not only that He would return, but that He would return for the express purpose of accompanying His followers back to Heaven!

But when will this occur? As graves are opened in that rural Central American cemetery, simultaneously they will be opening over the whole world. The body of every righteous person who ever lived will be resurrected, glorified and immortal, and reunited with the spirit and soul of he or she who used to inhabit it.

Never before, or ever again, will the earth and its inhabitants experience a moment such as this; every living person will either join the resurrected on their instantaneous journey to Heaven, or be left behind to endure mankind's darkest hour. For this is the moment of the next resurrection, and the rapture of...

FOUR

THE CHURCH: THE FOURTH RAPTURE

People who say the Church will not be raptured are in an unpleasant position. They believe the Church will experience the seven years of Tribulation and then, on that final day, at the seventh and last angelic trumpet, be taken to meet Christ in the air, only to come right back down with Him.

Such a belief does not seem reasonable to me. If there is no Rapture, we will never get to heaven. If we never get to heaven, a major portion of John's Revelation should be torn out and thrown away, because chapters four and five reveal events in heaven in which the Church must participate. In fact, there is no further reference to the Church until Revelation 19. The Wedding of the Lamb and the Marriage Supper are two events that take place in heaven, not on earth (See Rev. 19.). If the Church is to take part in these glorious events, it must be raptured *before* the Tribulation.

Someone has asked, "But doesn't Paul teach that we will be caught up *'in a moment, in the twinkling of an eye, at the last trump'* (1 Cor. 15:52)?" Yes, he does.

"Well, wouldn't that be the seventh angelic trumpet mentioned in Revelation 11?" No, it would not.

The seventh angelic trumpet of Revelation 11 does not sound until the final day of the Tribulation—the day Jesus comes back to earth. If there were seven years before the Church is taken to heaven, we would not be there to participate in any of the heavenly events revealed in Revelation. What, then, would we do with the heavenly events of the Wedding and Marriage Supper found in Revelation 19?

This is one of the great problems in the Church today. Many will not accept any reality in the Bible. To them, everything is interpreted figuratively! The devil is doing his best right now to strip away all reality from the Church and disguise everything in God's Word under a cloak of symbolism.

A Literal Event

Some things in Revelation are described in symbolic language, but certain events described in the Word are not to be taken figuratively or allegorically. They are foretold in literal terms and are meant to be taken literally. The catching away of the Church is a literal prophesied event.

The appearing of Jesus Christ in the heavens is a literal event. In John 14:3, Jesus makes this statement to His disciples, **"And if I go and prepare a place for you, *I will come again*, and receive you unto myself; *that where I am, there ye may be also.*"** Had He never gone away, we would have little reason to believe the rest of His statement. But He did go away as He said He would, and we have every reason to believe He will come again. One half of His prophecy was accurately fulfilled. Why doubt that the other half will be fulfilled?

Jesus said He would come again to receive us unto Himself. When He said that, He was speaking to His followers. *We* are His followers. He is coming back for *us*!

He said, **"I will come again, and receive you unto myself; that where I am** (please note the terminology), **there ye may be also."** This clearly indicates a change of position for us.

Jesus' appearing is literal; likewise, our being in heaven with Him is literal.

In 1 Corinthians 15:51-53, Paul wrote these words concerning the Rapture of the Church:

> **Behold, I shew you a mystery; We shall not all sleep** (die)**, but we shall all be changed, In a moment, in the twinkling of an eye,** *at the last trump: for the trumpet shall sound,* **and the dead shall be raised incorruptible, and we shall be changed.**
>
> **For this corruptible must put on incorruption, and this mortal must put on immortality.**

He also addresses this subject while writing to the Thessalonians:

> **For this we say unto you by the word of the Lord, that we which are alive and remain unto the** *coming of the Lord* **shall not prevent** (precede) **them which are asleep.**
>
> **For the Lord himself shall descend from heaven with a shout, with the voice of the archangel, and** *with the trump of God:* **and the dead in Christ shall rise first:**
>
> **Then we which are alive and remain shall be caught up together with them in the clouds to meet the Lord in the air: and so shall we ever be with the Lord.**
>
> **1 Thessalonians 4:15-17**

Notice that in both 1 Corinthians 15:51-53 and 1 Thessalonians 4:15-17, the rapture of the Church and the resurrection of all the righteous since Adam (the next resurrection) occur at the exact same time.

The Last Trumpet

Both times Paul refers to the last trumpet, or the trump of God. These are one and the same because the event is the same—the appearing of our Lord to catch away the righteous.

Study carefully the seventh angelic trumpet of Revelation 11 and you will make a discovery: the events surrounding the seventh trumpet are *not* the same as those surrounding the last trumpet of God. The last trumpet is God's final signal to welcome the Church into heaven.

If we were not going to be taken up until the sounding of the final angelic trumpet on the last day of the Tribulation Period, we would never get to heaven and participate in the heavenly events. We would not attend the Wedding of the Lamb and the Marriage Supper, or sing the new song, or witness Jesus opening the seals.

Jesus said of His appearing, **"Of that day and hour knoweth no man, no, not the angels of heaven, but my Father only"** (Matt. 24:36). Were we not caught up until the sounding of the seventh angelic trumpet on the final day of this seven-year period, anyone who had studied the Book of Revelation and chapter 14 of Zechariah would be able to calculate the very day and hour.

The final day of the seven-year period has a perfect chronological order from early morning to evening. Those seven years are a fixed period of time, exactly seven 360-day years—or 84 months, or 2,520 days—divided into two halves of 3½ years —or 42 months, or 1,260 days each.

Even if one were on earth during that period and did not get his countdown started at the beginning, he would have no problem calculating form midpoint. There the two witnesses from Jerusalem are counting down the days to Christ's return and His destruction of the Antichrist and the False Prophet (Rev. 11:1-13; 19:20). One could pick up on their countdown and know exactly what day Jesus would return to earth. The two witnesses are so powerful, you know the media will be covering them. The eleventh chapter of Revelation clearly indicates they will have been seen opposing the Antichrist worldwide.

Jesus said no one will know the day and hour of His appearing, but the day and hour of His return is clearly laid out in the Scriptures. The prophetic Scriptures (Zech. 14 and Rev. 19 and 20) tell of Christ's *return,* not His *appearing* to receive His Church! These are two separate and distinct events.

There is a major distinction between the "last trump," which is the "trumpet of God" heralding the Rapture of the Church, and the seventh angelic trumpet which precedes Christ's return to earth in judgment.

Since the Church will have already been raptured to heaven—the fourth rapture—it (the Church) will be prepared to return in triumph with Christ at His Second Coming, as stated in Zechariah 14:5 and Revelation 17:14 and 19:14.[1]

Understanding What the Bible Teaches
About the Rapture of the Church

To determine where the Rapture of the Church occurs in relation to the seven-year Tribulation Period, we need to look at Daniel 9:24-27 (See also 2 Thess. 2:1-9 and Rev. 4-5.). As we study these Scriptures, we will understand that this seven-year period cannot even begin as long as the Church is still on the earth.

Daniel's Prophecy of the End Time

Seventy weeks are determined upon thy people and upon thy holy city, to finish the transgression,

and to make an end of sins, and to make reconcilia-
tion for iniquity, and to bring in everlasting righteousness, and to seal up the vision and prophecy, and
to anoint the most Holy.

Know therefore and understand, that from the
going forth of the commandment to restore and to
build Jerusalem unto the Messiah the Prince shall be
seven weeks, and threescore and two weeks: the
street shall be built again, and the wall, even in trou-
blous times.

And after threescore and two weeks shall
Messiah be cut off, but not for himself: and the people of the prince that shall come shall destroy the city
and the sanctuary; and the end thereof shall be with
a flood, and unto the end of the war desolations are
determined.

And he shall confirm the covenant with many
for one week: and in the midst of the week he shall
cause the sacrifice and the oblation to cease, and for
the overspreading of abominations he shall make it
desolate, even until the consummation, and that
determined shall be poured upon the desolate.

Daniel 9:24-27

God is revealing His determined dealings with Israel. He
reveals to Daniel that it covers a period of seventy weeks, with
(each day a year) each week lasting seven years, making a total of
490 years. God also reveals to Daniel exactly when that period will
begin. He uses a fixed event which even secular history records:
the Persian king allowing Jewish slaves, led by Zerubbabel, Ezra
and Nehemiah to rebuild the city of Jerusalem. That is the signal
event which begins the 490-year period.

Then God reveals to Daniel that 483 of those years (or 69
full weeks) will be ended when the Messiah, the great Prince, is

"cut off" in Jerusalem (the Crucifixion). That leaves just one week, exactly seven years of the original period, to be fulfilled.

What Happened to the Final Week?
Why Has it Not Yet Been Fulfilled?

With the Crucifixion, God activated the Age of the Church. After 483 years of the 490 year span, God brought in the Church Age. Between the end of week 69 and the beginning of week 70 comes the era of the Church. God has left Himself only one week (seven years) after the Church Age in which to finish His direct dealings with Israel. It is during this time that all six major events of Daniel 9:24 must be fulfilled.

God originally gave Himself 490 years to accomplish these six events, yet 483 of those years have passed and He still has not accomplished them. That leaves only seven years for Him to fulfill the six prophecies on behalf of Israel. There is no doubt that He will do it. In fact, He has already begun the prelude to this fulfillment.

God is not only determined to have His way, but is patient. He will never force His will upon anyone, but patiently waits and works to cause them to accept His plan which is always better than their own.

In Daniel 9:26, 27, another prince comes on the scene and enters into agreement with Israel. This prince of Satan is the Antichrist. Satan can do nothing without a human being as his agent. According to Paul's second letter to the Thessalonians, this "man of sin" cannot be revealed to cause "the overspreading of abominations" until the Church has first been removed from the earth. Daniel places the beginning of Antichrist's activity at the onset of the last seven years of God's work with Israel.

Paul's Description of the Rapture

In 2 Thessalonians 2, Paul's writing cleared up some misconceptions that had arisen concerning the return of Christ to reign on earth. The Thessalonians were in a state of theological confusion. Paul had taught them correctly, but in his absence, someone else had come in, saying that Christ had already returned and that the day of Christ was "at hand."

Upon learning of their confusion and anxiety, Paul wrote a letter to set their thinking straight concerning the end times and the Lord's return. He speaks of the day of Christ and outlines the events which must precede that day:

> **Now we beseech you, brethren, by the coming of our Lord Jesus Christ, and by our gathering together unto him, That ye be not soon shaken in mind, or be troubled, neither by spirit, nor by word, nor by letter as from us, as that the day of Christ is at hand.**
>
> **Let no man deceive you by any means: for that day shall not come, except there come a falling away first, and that man of sin be revealed, the son of perdition; Who opposeth and exalteth himself above all that is called God, or that is worshipped; so that he as God sitteth in the temple of God, shewing himself that he is God.**
>
> **2 Thessalonians 2:1-4**

In verse 1, Paul talks about the day of Christ's appearing, at which time the Church is "gathered together unto Him." Then he goes on to say, "But you have become confused by those who have been teaching you that the day of Christ is at hand, that He has already returned and is here right now."

There are teachers today who teach that all Scriptures concerning the Second Coming are fulfilled when a person accepts Christ into his heart. They teach a figurative return of Christ, who comes back to earth spiritually by entering the hearts of believers.

Such teaching as this is one reason why you and I need to study the Word of God for ourselves! Nowhere in the Bible is there any indication that receiving Christ into your heart fulfills the Scriptures concerning either the appearing of Jesus or the Second Coming.

Some believe His appearing to be a spiritual thing. But we have seen in Acts 1:11 that when Jesus ascended bodily into heaven, there were angels standing among the Galileans who said to them, **"This same Jesus, which is taken up from you into heaven,** *shall so come in like manner as ye have seen him go into heaven."* That is not a spiritual thing; it is a reality!

The devil is trying to steal reality and, at the same time, steal the authority of the Scriptures. Twice the Apostle Paul speaks of comfort at just the thought of Christ's appearing (1 Thess. 4:18; 1 Thess. 5:11). Do not allow confused theology to steal your comfort.

Paul wrote to the Church in Thessalonica, "Someone has taught you mistakenly. He may have been a sincere man of God, but he has not taught you properly. I taught you correctly, that the day of Christ cannot come until first there be a "falling away" (or departure) and the 'man of sin' be revealed" (2 Thess. 2). If we stop at verse 4 of this chapter, Paul is teaching that Christ cannot come back to reign until there has been a "falling away" (or departure) and the "man of sin" has been revealed who exalts himself as God.

Let's read on:

> **Remember ye not, that, when I was yet with you, I told you these things?**
>
> **And now ye know what withholdeth that he** (the Antichrist) **might be revealed in his time.**
>
> **For the mystery of iniquity doth already work: only he who now letteth will let, until he be taken out of the way.**
>
> **And then shall that wicked be revealed, whom the Lord shall consume with the spirit of his mouth, and shall destroy with the brightness of his coming: even him, whose coming is after the working of Satan with all power and signs and lying wonders.**
>
> 2 Thessalonians 2:5-9

Paul states that the "man of sin," whom the Lord will destroy with the brightness of His coming, cannot be revealed to begin his activity, until that which has been withholding him has been taken out of the way (Verse 3 tells us plainly that the Antichrist must be revealed. Verse 6 declares that he is to be revealed *in his time.* His time is the fixed period of seven years, not part of the Church Age.) Something is restraining the Antichrist to keep him from coming forth prematurely. When that withholder, or restrainer, has been taken out of the way (and not one day sooner), then the "man of sin" will be revealed. He will be free to go about his evil activities until Christ comes to destroy him with the brightness of His coming at the end of the Tribulation.

The Church Restraining the Antichrist

And now ye know what withholdeth that he might be revealed in his time. For the mystery of iniquity doth already work: only he who now letteth will let, until

30

he be taken out of the way. And then shall that Wicked (one) **be revealed.**

2 Thessalonians 2: 6-7

Most of those who teach against the Rapture of the Church say this "restrainer" or "withholder," which is to be taken out of the way, is the Holy Spirit. But that is impossible for several reasons.

The Holy Ghost is God!

The unique character of God the Holy Ghost—the Third Person of the Trinity—allows Him to be present everywhere at all times. He cannot be "taken out" or "put in." The psalmist says of God;

Whither shall I go from thy spirit? Or whither shall I flee from thy presence? If I ascend up into heaven, thou art there: if I make my bed in hell, behold, thou art there.

Psalm 139:7-8

The Holy Spirit cannot be removed from the earth at anytime— not while the Church is still here, nor even after we depart!

If the Holy Ghost were to be taken so the Antichrist could be revealed to carry out his seven-year satanic plan, then nobody could be saved during that time. The Scripture says that no one comes to Jesus unless the Father draws him or her. He uses the Holy Ghost to bring about soul conviction (John 16:8; 6:44). How could God convict the world of sin if His Spirit had already departed? If God's Spirit had been removed from the earth, no one could be saved during the Tribulation.

The Church—that company of born-again, Spirit-filled, Spirit-led followers of Jesus; through whom God is working to reach the masses of people today—will be taken out of the way. The anointed Church is the restrainer, withholding unrestrained lawlessness in this hour.

Paul said, **"The mystery of iniquity doth already work"** (2 Thess. 2:7). The spirit of lawlessness, which is Satan's desire to bring forth the Antichrist, is already present. *The only thing withholding an eruption of lawlessness in the earth today, such as we have never seen, is the presence of the born-again Church of Jesus Christ!*

The Church, right now, is growing and getting stronger. Not only are we increasing in number, but we are learning more and more about the authority of God's Word and how to exercise that godly authority.

Believers must begin doing what the Word of God tells them to do with unswerving obedience; we will begin to see God's work advance and the works of the devil diminish!

From Joel chapter 2:28-31, we learn that once the Holy Spirit begins His earthly work through believers, that outpouring continues up to the final day of the Tribulation—the day when the sun becomes black and the moon becomes as blood (Matt. 24:29-30; Acts 2:16-21; Rev. 6:12-17). This is absolute proof that the Holy Spirit is not removed from the earth before the Tribulation. Therefore, the only other choice for removal is the anointed Church.

The Church in Heaven

In Revelation, chapters 4 and 5, the Apostle John describes the Church and all the righteous since Adam in heaven. The righteous of both the Old Testament and the New Testament are represented by the twenty-four elders.[2] Revelation chapters 4 and 5 are envisioned by Paul in Hebrews 12:22-24.

The full description of these twenty-four elders fits every believer. They have to be representatives because the number twenty-four is, itself, a symbolic figure. But even without the number twenty-four being symbolic of the righteous, the word *elder* alone is enough to indicate that this passage does not refer literally to only twenty-four men. In the New Testament, an elder always represents the Church before God and God to the Church. The twenty-four elders are not a company complete within themselves; they are just representatives of all the righteous caught up to Heaven.

The Church itself is mentioned in chapters 4 and 5 of Revelation. chapter 4 verse 6, refers to **"a sea of glass like unto crystal."** As a result of an intensive study of the Scriptures, I find the crystal sea to be a symbol of the Church and the Old Testament righteous before the throne of God. The verses before and after this passage make it evident that the word *"sea"* does not refer to a literal body of water, but rather symbolizes a mass of people. In fact, this is true throughout the Scriptures. Whenever the word *"sea"* is used in the Bible, unless it identifies a known body of water which can be located geographically, it always refers to a mass of people. In this particular case, it is called a **"crystal"** sea.

It is appropriate that John should symbolize the Church and Old Testament righteous as a crystal sea, because crystal is the only earthly substance in which a flaw cannot go undetected. Flaws in other substances—diamonds, rubies, sapphires, emeralds, platinum, gold, silver, fine brass—may be hidden, but not in crystal. The nature of crystal is such that it magnifies a flaw. As a collector of crystal, particularly antique cut glass, I can verify this. John chose well his symbol of the Church. Paul wrote in Ephesians 5:27 that when Jesus presents the Church to Himself, it will be a **"glorious church, not having spot, or wrinkle, or any such thing; but that it should be holy and *without blemish*."**

So we find the Church in heaven just as Paul said it would have to be before the Antichrist could begin his activity. Daniel said the Antichrist would start work at the beginning of the seven-year period. In 2 Thessalonians, we see that the Antichrist cannot begin his activity until the withholding factor is taken out of the way. By properly analyzing these Scriptures, with the help of the Holy Spirit, we discover that "the withholder" is the Church of Jesus Christ.

Revelation, chapters 4 and 5 describe God on His throne along with the Holy Spirit, four awesome angels, Jesus, and the righteous who have been caught up. The Church is there *with all of the angels.* This is significant because in Hebrews 1:14 we learn that angels are **"ministering spirits, sent forth to minister for them who shall be heirs of salvation"**—in other words, *us!*

Angels are on direct assignment from God to minister for those who shall be called heirs of salvation. The angels have proven their loyalty go God; they will not fail on their assignment.

Since John pictures *all* of the angels in heaven before the throne of God, the Church would have to be there also. Otherwise, the Church would be left on earth without the "ministering spirits." If the Church were still here, then the angels would still be here too, right where they are at this moment, taking care of their ministry assignment on our behalf.

John tells us in Revelation 5:11, **"the number of them** (the angels) **was ten thousand times ten thousand, and thousands of thousands."** Since 100 billion angels are in heaven, all at the same time, that means everybody they had been assigned to protect or to minister to would be there also.

The Antichrist Released

And I saw when the Lamb opened one of the seals, and I heard, as it were the noise of thunder, one of the four beasts saying, Come and see.
And I saw, and behold a white horse: and he that sat on him had a bow; and a crown was given unto him: and he went forth conquering, and to conquer.
Revelation 6:1-2

At this juncture, Jesus opens the first seal of the scroll He has taken from His Father's hand. When He opens the seal, the man destined to be the Antichrist is released. According to Daniel 9:24-27, this occurs at the beginning of the seven-year period known as the Tribulation. Therefore the exact time for Jesus to open the first seal is revealed.

Several things must take place before the Antichrist can begin his activity. The righteous Church has to be taken up to heaven to stand before the throne of God, observing as Jesus opens the first seal. When it is opened, the Antichrist is released. If Jesus never opened that first seal, the Antichrist could never begin his evil activity, whether we were up there or not. But Jesus will not open the seal until we are there. Our departure to heaven and the opening of the first seal both reveal and release the Antichrist.

To confirm what I have just described, let's look at Hebrews 12:22-24:

> **But ye are come unto mount Sion, and unto the city of the living God, the heavenly Jerusalem and to an innumerable company of angels,**
>
> **To the general assembly and church of the firstborn, which are written in heaven, and to God the Judge of all, and to the spirits of just men made perfect, And to Jesus the mediator of the New covenant, and to the blood of sprinkling, that speaketh better things than that of Abel.**

We find Paul describing the same scene in heaven that John has described in chapters 4 and 5 of Revelation. In three verses, Paul gives a descriptive outline that takes John two full chapters to relate. But it confirms, that at the same time, *all* the angels are in heaven *the general assembly and church of the firstborn are also there.* Praise God!

The Second Coming of Jesus

No other subject in the Word of God is more exciting and important to a child of God than the appearing in glory of our Savior and Lord (See Titus 2:13.)

We are, of course, excited about the wonderful salvation that is ours through the Lord Jesus Christ and the marvelous infilling of the Holy Spirit that so many believers around the world are enjoying. But it is equally exciting to know that when Jesus Christ, the Son of God, appears in the heavens, the resurrection of all the righteous since Adam will occur; then the living members of the true Church will be caught up from the earth with the angels. We then will be escorted to meet Christ in the air and proceed with Him to the throne of God.

It is also exciting to know that Jesus Christ will return to establish His government here on earth. The prophecies of Isaiah 9:6 will be fulfilled: **"The government shall be upon His shoulder."** But before He can take the government upon His shoulder, He must appear and receive the Church unto Himself. *These two events—His appearing and His return to reign on earth—make up the Second Coming of Jesus.*

When you hear ministers speaking about the Second Coming, listen closely. Most of the time, they are actually referring to His appearing to catch up His Church, and not to His return to earth. I hear little teaching or preaching about the actual return of Christ to reign on earth. Most ministers today are looking for the appearing of Jesus; so they talk about the Second Coming in relation to His appearing. But these are two distinct events. Let's not misuse the terms and thereby confuse the Church.

There has been a great amount of confusion about this subject in the past, due to a lack of knowledge and understanding of God's Word. However, we are now in a blessed time when the

Holy Spirit is opening our understanding to some exciting truths. Confusion over the rapture (catching away) of the righteous is a work of Satan. 1 Corinthians 14:33 clearly states, **"God is not the author of confusion."**

I believe you will be able to see the distinction between the appearing of the Lord Jesus Christ to catch away the righteous Church, and His return to the earth with all the righteous, as we study these two events in the Word. A fixed period of seven years separate the two events. Both must take place because they have been prophesied, not only by sincere prophets of God, but also by the Lord Jesus Himself.

Let us consider His appearing. In the sequence of events, the appearing takes place first.

Jesus' Appearing Before the Tribulation

The book of Revelation makes it clear that at the appearing of the Lord Jesus Christ, the righteous will be caught up unto Him and will not be on earth during the seven years of Tribulation. Chapter 4 verses 1 and 2 harmonize beautifully with 1 Thessalonians 4:16-18 and Luke 21:36.

In the words of Jesus, and in the writings of Paul, we as members of the true Church are admonished to watch and pray, to look for His appearing, and to keep ourselves in a state of readiness. God's Word clearly defines His glorious appearing, so there need not be any further confusion concerning it. There are many references in the Scriptures regarding this sudden and glorious appearing of the Lord Jesus Christ. These Scriptures admonish us to be ready, vigilant, sober, watching, and praying. Christ's appearing *is* going to happen, and what an exciting event it will be! (Matt. 24:44; 25:13; Mark 13:32-37; Luke 21:28,36: Heb. 9:28; Titus 2:13)

The prime responsibility of the Holy Spirit today is to get the Church ready so that at the moment of His appearing, as the Apostle Paul wrote in Ephesians 5:27, the Church will be without spot, wrinkle, or blemish.[4]

For the Church to be ready for this event, it will require a great amount of *ministry* by apostles, prophets, evangelists, pastors, and teachers. In Ephesians 4 the Apostle Paul states that the Church is perfected, not through tribulation and trial, but through the God-given, Holy Spirit-anointed *ministry* of apostles, prophets, evangelists, pastors, and teachers.

But this perfection will only come if we Christians are willing to receive ministry. If one is not willing, then he or she may expect much buffeting from our adversary, the devil—all because of a lack of knowledge of God's Word. We must take advantage of the ministry God has provided for us. I urge you to get into a study of God's Word and receive the proven ministry of those who labor among you, those who come highly recommended by reputable men of God. If your pastor is indeed called by God and ministers the Word with Holy Spirit anointing, he is extremely important to your spiritual growth.

Some people reason that the Rapture will not happen. After all, they say, we are human, and as humans we could not survive a trip through the stratosphere without oxygen. Any person who says this is totally unaware of New Testament teachings concerning the glorious transformation that takes place when the Lord appears to receive His own unto Himself (1 John 3:1-3).

Others say that if the Rapture does occur it will not take place until the close of the Great Tribulation. Those who teach this are saying that we will rise to meet Jesus in the air, then come right back with Him. They have a limited knowledge of God's Word, particularly of the Book of Revelation. Revelation makes it clear that there are many activities in which the Church must participate in heaven, such as the Wedding of the Lamb, followed by the Marriage Supper. According to Revelation 19, both events take place in heaven during the Tribulation Period. Since we have to participate in those heavenly events, we will have to be taken there. One cannot participate in these heavenly events unless he or she is present. We have learned from biblical references the only way to get to heaven bodily is by rapture.

Zechariah and Revelation make it clear that when Christ returns to earth to rule the governments of the world, those who have been in heaven will return with Him (Zech.14:5; Rev. 17:14; 19:14).

Revelation also reveals that the man who has become the Antichrist not only blasphemes God and His tabernacle, but **"them that dwell in heaven"** (Rev. 13:5,6). How did "them that dwell in heaven" get there without a rapture—or catching up? Teachers may reason that these are the spirits and souls of the dead in Christ. We would be naïve to use one passage of Scripture as a cover for our lack of understanding. Let's allow the whole of God's Word to speak to this subject.

If you search for a single verse of Scripture which states specifically that the appearing of the Lord Jesus Christ and the catching up of the Church is prior to the Tribulation, your search will be in vain. There is no such verse. But by studying the whole of God's Word (which you should do), you will discover that the appearing of the Lord Jesus Christ is a certainty. The taking up of the Church to meet Him in the air is for sure, and it very definitely comes before the Tribulation can begin.

You will want to go back and read this again and again until these marvelous truths are yours. You will then be able to share the truth with many other believers who are distressed and filled with despair; not knowing if the Lord is coming and, if He is, whether it will be prior to the Tribulation; they are concerned and confused.

Multitudes of people lack an understanding of this subject, wondering if the "poor Church" will have to "suffer through the trials of the Great Tribulation."

Know the Truth

Some of the most negative teachings you can imagine have been presented on the "Tribulation suffering of the Church."

I proclaim that the Church is in the driver's seat. *From now until the appearing of Jesus, the Church of Jesus Christ is to become the strongest and most outstanding influence upon the face of the earth!* Check it out in God's Word and see for yourself. Realize that the prayers Jesus prayed[5] are going to come to pass. The statements He made concerning the Church (as declared in Matthew 16:18 where He said He would build His Church and the gates of hell would not prevail against it) are going to be fulfilled. You and I are already beginning to experience these things.

I want you to be absolutely convinced that He is going to appear. Unless you have that fact firmly fixed in your mind, there is little reason for you to be concerned about the Second Coming.

We find within the teachings of the Apostle Paul that he is very emphatic about our being informed so that day should not come upon us unaware (1 Thess. 5:1-11). The Word of God is our source of information about this appearing, not dreams, visions, or revelations, but God's Word. When there are dreams, visions, and revelations, they must be judged by the Word and found to be in harmony with the Word. If they are not, we do not give them any consideration.

Consider this Bible truth found in Genesis chapter six. The biblical account of the flood further establishes that the righteous are taken up before the Tribulation.

Our God and His ways are perfect. Once God does a certain thing in a certain way, He will not ever change His method (Mal. 3:6; James 1:17). The ark in Genesis chapter six was an Old Testament type of the Rapture. It bore the righteous above the wrath of God and kept them there until His wrath (the flood) subsided. When so, they were once again placed here on the Earth. This is a perfect Old Testament picture of the truth as taught by Jesus and Paul.

Since God is perfect, He always removes the righteous before the use of His wrath. Examine these Bible references: Nahum 1:2; Romans 5:9; 1 Thess. 1:10; and 1 Thess. 5:9-10.

A Cause for Excitement

In John 14:1-3, Jesus said:

> **Let not your heart be troubled: you believe in God, believe also in me.**
> **In my Father's house are many mansions: if it were not so, I would have told you.**
> **I go to prepare a place for you. And if I go and prepare a place for you, I will come again, and** *receive you unto myself*; **that where I am, there you may be also.**

This is a thrilling passage of Scripture, especially in this time when people everywhere are distressed. Jesus said, **"Let not your heart be troubled."** He said, "Believe in Me, even as you have believed in God." This is God's cure for a troubled heart. Jesus was speaking to Jews who had trusted in God but were having difficulty accepting Him.

He also spoke this to His followers, but they did not yet have full spiritual understanding of Him or His teachings.

The answer to the many perplexing problems and the great stress and strain of today is Jesus—nothing else—not money, social status, psychiatry, New Age, or even religion. People today are experimenting with all kinds of religion, but the answer is not there. The answer is in Jesus Christ, the Son of God, who came and shed His blood so that you and I might have life and have it more abundantly (see John 10:10). These truths edify and thrill one's soul and spirit!

Jesus said in John 14:2-3, **"I go to prepare a place for you. And if I go and prepare a place for you, I will come again, and** *receive you unto myself;* **that where I am,** *there you may be also."* This is an important verse of Scripture. Jesus told the disciples that He was going to prepare a place for them, and that when He did, He would come back and receive them unto Himself.

He did go away, and we have the record of His ascension in Acts 1:9. Since that much of the prophetic statement is already fulfilled, we have every reason to believe the rest will come to pass. We know He went away and we know He sits at the right hand of the Father, interceding for us and serving as our High Priest (See Rom. 8:34; Heb. 4:14.). We also know He said, **"I will come again"** (John 14:3).

What is He going to do on the occasion of His appearing? He said, "I will receive you unto myself." His words do not indicate that He is going to come here and abide with us. The key word is *receive,* which, in the Greek, means "to take" or "to receive beside."

His words do not at all imply that He will come and abide here with us or that we are going to be given some special place of hiding during the Tribulation. Many teachers confuse the Church with the remnant of Revelation, chapter 12. The thought that the Church is to be hidden away is an absolute misapplication of God's Word. By carefully studying the Book of Revelation, you will find that it is the remnant of Israel—not the Church—which is placed in hiding for three and one-half years.

We understand that we are to be received beside Him. This agrees with Jesus' other teachings on this subject. In Revelation 3:21, He said, **"To him that overcometh will I grant *to sit with me in my throne*, even as I also overcame, and am set down with my Father in his throne."** Since we are to sit in His throne in heaven, He will have to receive us to Himself.

Jesus concludes His statement about receiving us unto Himself: **"that where I am** (not *where you are*, but *where I am*), **there you may be also."** We know where He is and we are looking forward to being with Him in that very place. In this passage of Scripture, Jesus makes it clear that He is coming back to receive us—His followers, the Church—unto Himself, so that where He is, *there* we may be also.

He spoke these things when the Church had not yet been established. He was in the process of laying the foundation of the Church and He was to become the chief cornerstone. He was telling the disciples that, after the process had been completed and the Church had reached its glorious position, He would come and receive it unto Himself.

If there were nothing else in God's Word about His appearing and the events that are to take place at that time, this one passage would be enough to establish these truths. Yet there is more.

Lift Up Your Heads

And when these things begin to come to pass, then *look up*, and *lift up your heads*; for your redemption draweth nigh.

Luke 21:28

At His appearing, Jesus will not come down to earth. He will appear in the immediate heavens and catch the righteous up unto Himself. The Holy Spirit and angels will play a major role in this event. Angels were involved in both Elijah's translation and the taking up of Jesus, and they will also be involved when the Church is caught up.

> **And while they looked steadfastly toward heaven as he went up, behold, two men stood by them in white apparel; which also said, Ye men of Galilee, why stand ye gazing up into heaven? This same Jesus, which is taken up from you into heaven, shall so come in like manner as ye have seen him go into heaven.**
>
> **Acts 1:10-11**

The disciples were not able to understand this and they inquired of Jesus, saying, **"Master, but when shall these things be? And what sign will there be when these things shall come to pass?"** (Luke 21:7).

In order to answer their questions, Jesus took upon Himself the office of a prophet. This was necessary because their questions dealt with future events. The prophetic answers, given by Jesus, covered a vast time frame which included the Church Age and our generation.

Allow me to point out that Matthew 24, Mark 13, and Luke 21 are "sister" chapters. These chapters are often referred to as the "Olivet Discourse," and came about as a result of the questions asked by the disciples in Matthew 24:3

In Luke 21:28, Jesus points out the proper attitude of a believing follower. **"And when these things *begin to come to pass*, then *look up*, and *lift up your heads*; for your redemption draweth nigh."**

44

The signs Jesus gave in Luke 21, which would BEGIN to come to pass were:

1) Jerusalem is no longer controlled by Gentiles.
2) Fear becomes a killer, causing heart failure.
3) Men (through the space program) create signs in the heavens.
4) Nations distressed and perplexed due to the upheaval of masses (of people).

These prophecies did not come to pass in the days of the disciples, but surely we are seeing them fulfilled in this generation. It was not until after the disciples received the infilling of the Holy Spirit that they were able to understand Jesus' teachings of the spiritual kingdom, His appearing, and His eventual return to earth to establish His earthly kingdom. This shows how vitally important the infilling of the Holy Spirit is to our understanding of God's Word.

So Jesus speaks to us today. He says, **"Be excited but not alarmed. When these things begin to come to pass, look up and know that your redemption is at hand."** This does not mean to walk around with your head turned toward the sky, but to maintain a proper attitude, a spiritual awareness of what is about to happen.

Jesus said we will see things beginning to come to pass. The emphasis is on the "beginning," not on the end, when all has been fulfilled. If Jesus did not appear to receive the Church until the end of the Tribulation, all things pertaining to that period would have been fulfilled. Our study of Luke 21 teaches us to look for His appearing when prophecies *begin* to be fulfilled—not at the end of the Tribulation, but before it. When we see these things *beginning* to come to pass, we are to look up, for our redemption draws nigh. The final act of redemption is the glorification of the physical body (See 1 John 3:2; Heb. 9:28; Luke 21:28.).

Bible prophecies are rapidly being fulfilled. Everything happening in our world is pointing to the appearing of our Lord and Savior Jesus Christ.

We need to obey the Word and begin to look for His appearing, lifting up our heads from the despair, confusion, negativism, and defeat which has ensnared so many in the church for years.

It's time to recognize that our redemption—the final work of the salvation purchased for us at Calvary—is about to be completed. At His appearing, we will be caught up and our bodies will experience the final application of salvation: when mortality puts on immortality and corruption puts on incorruption (1 Cor.15:51-53).

We are admonished that when we see things beginning to come to pass (such as the re-establishment of the nation of Israel, particularly the retaking of the city of Jerusalem; the space program now probing the heavens; and the many problems that have brought such distress to the governments of the world), we are to look up and lift up our heads, for our redemption draws nigh (Luke 21:28).

Jesus teaches us that the generation which experiences the restoration of Israel (the fig tree[6]) will also experience the appearing of Jesus (Matt 24:32-34; Mark 13:28-30; Luke 21:29-32). I believe his appearing could occur in our lifetime.

Watch and Pray

In Luke 21:36, Jesus says, **"Watch ye therefore, and pray always, that ye may be accounted worthy to escape all these things that shall come to pass, and to stand before the Son of Man."** It is important to understand this verse of Scripture. Jesus said to watch. That means we should not be slumbering or sleeping, or in other words, not apathetic. Neither are we to become weighted down with the heaviness of teachings that, instead of edifying, place us in despair, fear, and negativism. We are to watch and pray, so that we may be **"accounted worthy to escape all these things that shall come to pass."** The key word here is *escape*.

I have heard people say that escapism is not for them, that they will trust God. That is a strange statement to make, considering the word *escape* is actually used by Jesus. It is even found in the original language from which the Scriptures are translated. Paul also uses "escape" in Hebrews 2:3. To neglect one's salvation is to cut off one's way of escape.

Although Jesus tells us in Luke 21:36 that we can **"escape all these things that shall come to pass and stand before the Son,"** escaping the Tribulation is the effect of, not the purpose of, the Rapture. In fact, the Church has no <u>need</u> whatsoever to escape anything. We are already more than conquerors (Rom. 8:37), Jesus always causes us to triumph (2 Cor. 2:14), and we can do all things through Christ who strengthens us (Phil. 4:13). Furthermore, **"greater is He who is in us than he who is in the world"** (1 John 4:4), and we are practicing overcomers (1 John 2:13 & 14; 4:4; 5:4 & 5; Rev. 2:7,11, 26; 3:5, 12, 21; 21:7).

The Church—like Enoch, Elijah and Jesus before us— will be raptured after gloriously completing our ministry assignment here on the Earth (2 Tim. 4:8).

The Trumpet we will hear (1 Thess. 4:16; 1 Cor. 15:52; Rev. 4:1) will be welcoming the victorious army of living, soul-winning saints along with all the righteous since Adam whose souls and spirits have just been reunited with their resurrected, glorified bodies. At that moment, our Lord Jesus will have completed another phase of His victory over death.

Jesus said, "Watch and pray that you might be accounted worthy." Do we consider ourselves worthy? If not, what can we do to make ourselves worthy? Our own righteousness will never avail, but His will. We need to realize that we are righteous because He is righteous. Paul tells us in 2 Corinthians 5:20-21: **"We pray you in Christ's stead, be ye reconciled to God. For he** (God) **hath made him** (Christ) **to be sin for us, who knew no sin; that** *we might be made the righteousness of God in him.*"

Our righteousness, holiness, and sanctification are based in Him. Jesus makes it very clear that watching and praying will contribute to our being worthy. Remember, God keeps the books and He is evaluating our spiritual lives. We are judged by Him, not by our peers.

As we carefully observe Bible prophecies being fulfilled we become all the more aware of the coming of Jesus. The thought of His coming should comfort us. When we pray, we enter into communion with our heavenly Father. Prayer can be a two-way conversation, if we allow it.

What a blessing it is to find ourselves in a relationship with God the Father, God the Son, and God the Holy Ghost. Watching and praying are two important things God's children are to do.

Because of the wonderful relationship we have with God, we recognize that we are worthy. It really is not complicated, but is a simple matter of doing what Jesus instructs: "Watch and pray." When we do what we are told, we will be rewarded. The reward is to escape **all** the things that shall come to pass—not to just "endure" or "make it through," but to *escape.* The word *escape* does not imply "to be protected in," but rather "to quickly go out from." *We are not going to be protected during the Tribulation; we are going to escape it!* Read carefully 1 Thessalonians 5:1-11. The Rapture is *an escape from God's wrath!* Literally a removal so God can begin the use of His wrath.

I am sorry for those who do not believe in the catching up of the Church. They have to disbelieve or explain away more Scriptures than they use to support their erroneous belief. In some instances, verses are taken out of the original setting, changing how they relate to the rest of the Scriptures. To do this only causes confusion. Sound teaching always edifies, blesses, and is harmonious with all other Scriptures.

The word *escape* implies a quick action. God's Word teaches us from many passages that so shall His appearing be:

"In the twinkling of an eye (1 Cor. 15:52). **Immediately I was in the spirit: and, behold, a throne was set in heaven** (Rev. 4:2). **As a thief in the night** (1 Thess. 5:2).**"**

We are admonished to be ready on a daily basis. It is not something we do today that lasts from now on. We simply keep ourselves in a state of daily readiness, watching for His glorious appearing, so that we may be caught up to meet Him in the air and stand in His holy presence at the throne of God.

By the way, soul winning will help keep you ready and wise.

Jesus' Appearing at the Sound of the Trump

Another passage of Scripture which tells of our Lord's appearing is 1 Corinthians 15:51. The Apostle Paul writes: **"Behold, I shew you a mystery; We shall not all sleep** (die), **but we shall all be changed."**

Paul reveals that believers who are asleep (the dead in Christ) will be resurrected, which points out the doctrine of resurrection. Also, the statement establishes that there will be many believers living at the time of the event; and both the resurrected and living saints will be changed, pointing to the moment of physical glorification.

Many recognize that Paul was expecting the imminent return of Jesus during his lifetime, since he exhorted the Church to be ready and remain ready for the Rapture (See 1 Cor. 15:52; Heb. 2:1-3; 9:28; 12:22-24; Phil. 3:20.). Besides this revelation, he also knew of Jesus' teachings (John 14:3; Luke 21:36; Matt. 25:10; Luke 12:35-40) and that no one could know the day and hour of His appearing (See Matt. 24:36.). He knew God was a God of order and would not send Jesus for the Church until that event came up in the prophetic process.

As an Old Testament scholar, Paul knew that before Jesus could receive the Church, the nation of Israel would have to be restored. The Holy Spirit revealed that the Church itself would have to be mature, united, and glorious before the catching up. Since the Holy Spirit could have possibly brought about these events in his lifetime, Paul exhorted the Church to prepare for Jesus' appearing. He also knew that if these events did not occur during his lifetime, they would occur in the time of other believers.

We are those other believers, because prophecies pertaining to the restoration of the nation of Israel are being fulfilled in our time.

Paul continues in 2 Corinthians 15:52, **"In a moment, *in the twinkling of an eye*, at the last trump."** The Rapture is a quick action, a sudden event, not drawn out; it will come as a thief in the night (1 Thess. 5:1-11).

"For the trumpet (the last trump) **shall sound, and the dead shall be raised incorruptible, and we shall be changed"** (v. 52). Paul, by the Holy Spirit, reveals the dead in Christ being raised incorruptible and the living saints being changed. Paul was still alive at this time, so he was including himself among those who were living in Christ, not the dead in Christ.

The Last Trump

This verse is often used by those who teach that the Church will not be caught up until the end of the Tribulation. They say the last trump is the seventh trumpet of the Book of Revelation, Chapter 11. Such teaching is erroneous. The seventh angelic trumpet in Revelation is not the same trumpet described by the Apostle Paul in 1 Corinthians 15:51-53 and in 1 Thessalonians 4:16-17.

Verse 16 says, **"For the Lord himself shall descend from heaven with a shout, with the voice of the archangel, and with the trump of God: and the dead in Christ shall rise first."** This is exactly what Paul said in 1 Corinthians 15:52, that the dead shall be raised incorruptible.

Now look at verse 17: **"Then we which *are alive and remain* shall be caught up together with them in the clouds, to meet the Lord in the air."**

It is amazing, but true, that the descriptions of the events surrounding the sounding of Paul's trumpets are one and the same (See 1 Cor. 15:52-53 and 1 Thess. 4:16-17.). How very beautiful and exciting! At the sounding of that trumpet, the dead in Christ will be resurrected and the living saints will be changed and caught up to meet Jesus in the air.

Some say, "But it's the *last* trumpet." Yes. However, Paul further elaborates in 1 Thessalonians 4:16 that this is the trumpet of God, not an angelic trumpet. These two must not be confused. All seven trumpets in the Book of Revelation are angelic trumpets which release some part of God's wrath or bring about events involving the Tribulation Period. (The Church will not have any part in the Tribulation Period, as a study of the whole of God's Word bears out.)

In 1 Corinthians 15, and 1 Thessalonians 4, Paul is writing about the trumpet of God. Trumpet calls are mentioned a number of times in the Scriptures. In these references, God uses His trumpet as part of the welcome for the conquering and overcoming, righteous Church. What a glorious event that will be! The dead in Christ will be raised and the living saints will be caught up together with them in the clouds to meet the Lord in the air.

1 Thessalonians 4:18 says, **"Wherefore comfort one another with these words."** The word *comfort* could be interpreted "exhort one another." The appearing of the Lord Jesus Christ, the resurrection of the dead in Christ, the catching up of the living saints, all rising in the clouds to meet Him in the air is an exhilarating truth that strengthens and excites us. When someone teaches that it is not going to happen—that the Word really does not mean that—it fills one with despair and fails to edify.

I have observed Christians who listen to teachings contrary to the Word who seem so burdened. They have no joy and little or no evangelistic vision. They wonder, "When will we have to go into the Tribulation Period? It's going to be so bad!"

Someone else will say, "Oh, it's not going to be so bad, because we know our God is going to keep us through it all."

How long is it going to take the Church of Jesus Christ to realize the thrilling truth that God is keeping us every day? We do not have to go into the Tribulation to find out about the power God has to keep us. Let Him do it now and enjoy it! Look forward to the time when Christ will appear and catch us up to meet Him in the air.

We have seen that the trump of God, as described in 1 Corinthians 15 and 1 Thessalonians 4, is not the same trumpet as described by John in Revelation 11. The seventh trumpet in Revelation 11 is blown by an angel to signal God's wrath. It does not have the same significance or serve the same purpose as the one described by the Apostle Paul.

The seventh angelic trumpet signals the end of the Tribulation Period, the beginning of the Battle of Armageddon, and the return of Jesus to earth. The Books of Zechariah and Revelation declare that the saints are returning to earth with Him. If they had not been in heaven with Him, how could they return?

When people ask about certain verses in Matthew 24 and 2 Thessalonians 2, I tell them to allow these passages to relate to the whole of the Bible. I've had them say, "But that changes the meaning." Whose meaning? Certainly not God's. Never take a passage of Scripture out of context. Remember, the Bible interprets itself, if given the opportunity. However, one must study the whole Word to discover its truths.

Watch Therefore

1 Corinthians 15:52 describes the *last* trumpet. Let me emphasize that the description of the events at the sounding of this trumpet is not the same as the description of the events at the sounding of the seventh angelic trumpet in Revelation 11. This is the *trumpet of God.* It will be sounded by God, not an angel. It has nothing to do with the Tribulation, but has everything to do with the closing of the Church Age and the righteous being caught up.

In 1 Thessalonians 4:17, the key phrase is *caught up.* In the Greek, it simply means "to snatch away." Though some do not believe in the "Great Snatch," that is what this Scripture teaches. I believe in the "Great Snatch" because that is exactly what the Apostle Paul is teaching.

If nothing were going to happen, Jesus would not have pointed out that we ought to be sober and vigilant, watching, praying, and working in the harvest fields. Something is going to happen to those who are really involved and committed. One should be delighted to know exactly what the Word of God has to say. There is no way to refute it without changing the Word—there *will* be a catching up.

The Ten Virgins

Another passage of Scripture which supports the appearing of the Lord Jesus Christ is Matthew 25:1-13, the parable of the ten virgins:

> **Then shall the kingdom of heaven be likened unto ten virgins, which took their lamps, and went forth to meet the bridegroom. And five of them were wise, and five were foolish.**
>
> **They that were foolish took their lamps, and took no oil with them: but the wise took oil in their vessels with their lamps.**
>
> **While the bridegroom tarried, they all slumbered and slept.**
>
> **And at midnight there was a cry made, Behold, the bridegroom cometh; go ye out to meet him.**
>
> **Then all those virgins arose, and trimmed their lamps. And the foolish said unto the wise, Give us of your oil; for our lamps are gone out. But the wise answered, saying, Not so; lest there be not enough for us and you: but go ye rather to them that sell, and buy for yourselves.**
>
> **And while they went to buy, the bridegroom came; and *they that were ready went in with him* to the marriage: and the door was shut.**
>
> **Afterward came also the other virgins, saying, Lord, Lord, open to us. But he answered and said, Verily I say unto you, I know you not.**
>
> **Watch therefore, for ye know neither the day nor the hour wherein the Son of man cometh.**

The wise virgins were ready. Matthew 25:10 says that while the foolish virgins went to make their purchase, the Bridegroom came. Those who were ready (the wise virgins) went in with Him to the marriage and the door was shut. The key phrase is *they went in with Him* to the marriage. The Bridegroom did not come where they were; they were escorted by Him.

In John 14:3, the Lord said He would come again to receive us unto Himself so that where He is, *there* we may be also. 1 Corinthians 15 and 1 Thessalonians 4 tie in with John 14:3 because there is going to be a meeting in the air, and we are going to be where He is.

The Bridegroom did not come to the place where the virgins were to give them special keeping or help in their time of trouble. They (who were ready) went in with Him to the marriage.

According to Revelation 19, the marriage ceremony of the Lamb is a heavenly event, not an earthly one. It must take place in heaven before the throne of God. We will be caught up to participate in heavenly events before God's throne. This further convinces me that there is going to be an appearing of Jesus and that we will be caught up and escorted by Him to heaven.

I exhort you in earnest: don't play games with God and don't play "church." Get involved with what the Holy Spirit is doing today. Allow Him to work in your life on a daily basis and keep you ready for the appearing of Jesus. Don't fall into the category of those who would be called *foolish* because they were not ready. This does not mean they were not a part of the Church (there is every indication that they were) or that they were lost; it means they missed the Rapture. Do not be a person who attempts to serve God out of religious habit, but serve Him out of love for Him.

I am not teaching a split Rapture, but I believe it is possible for a child of God to miss the Rapture if he becomes foolish about his relationship with the Lord. Foolish Christians will not necessarily be lost, but they certainly will not meet the Lord in the air. Those who are left will endure part of the Tribulation and will have to take advantage of the other vehicle for leaving this earth which, according to Revelation, is provided during the Tribulation. Study Revelation 7:9-17 and you will see how very clear this truth is.

In 1 Thessalonians 5:9-10, the Apostle Paul gives further insight into the appearing of the Lord Jesus Christ and the fact that we will not participate in anything on earth after that event. The scripture states:

For God hath not appointed us to wrath, but to obtain salvation by our Lord Jesus Christ, who died for us, that, whether we wake or sleep, we should live together with him.

This agrees with what Paul writes in 1 Thessalonians 4 and, 1 Corinthians 15:51-52. Whether we are the dead in Christ or living saints, we shall live together with Him. We are not appointed to wrath but to complete salvation. The final act of salvation is the glorification of our bodies at the appearing of the Lord Jesus Christ, when we are caught up to meet Him in the air. Then we go with Him to appear before God's throne in heaven.

The key words in 1 Thessalonians 5:9 are *"not appointed."* Paul was instructing the Church that we are not appointed to wrath but to obtain salvation by our Lord Jesus Christ. There are those who teach that the Church will be here during the Tribulation and that God will provide perfect keeping for it. I understand this reasoning, but because it is not scripturally sound, I cannot accept it. Examine carefully 1 Thessalonians 1:10 and Romans 5:9. These verses are very clear in their meaning.

Watch—Pray—Escape

Look again at Luke 21:36: **"Watch ye therefore, and pray always, that ye may be accounted worthy to escape all these things that shall come to pass, and to stand before the Son of man."**

Watch is a word of action involving commitment, alertness, and readiness, while *prayer* is "communication with God." Proper communication releases great power. These two assignments, properly carried out, equate to *worthiness*. Jesus said, **"Those who are worthy will escape all that *shall* come to pass."**

If you are a committed person of prayer, accept the benefits of your obedience. You *are* worthy—worthy to *escape* all things that shall come to pass (that's future) and be received by Jesus to stand with Him in heaven at God's throne (See John 14:3.).

Notice Jesus said *escape all*. We who are worthy are to escape *all*—not part, but all—of the things of the future, once the Church Age is concluded. If we were not to be caught up until the end of the Tribulation to escape that which follows, we would escape the one thousand reign as kings and priests (See Rev. 2:26, 27; 5:10.). So we escape the trials, troubles, and tribulations which are coming on the earth.

Also look at the experience of John, recorded in Revelation 4:1,2. Notice John's description of his experience. It parallels the event of 1 Thessalonians 4:16,17 which takes place before God reveals what is to come, with Luke 21:36, and the two are in perfect harmony.

When one carefully studies the Book of Revelation, a discovery is made: the Tribulation Period cannot begin until the first seal of Revelation 6:1-2 is opened by Jesus. When this event occurs at God's throne, the Church is standing there observing it (Rev. 5:9-10).

Let's examine another passage of Scripture concerning the appearing of Jesus. In Revelation 3, the Lord Jesus Christ dictates a letter to John, for the church at Philadelphia. He did not rebuke the Philadelphian Christians or call to their attention anything that displeased Him. They were getting the job done. This church had an open door, an outreach, and anointing. The important thing about the Philadelphians was that they kept the Word of God.

In verse 10, the Lord says, **"Because thou hast kept the word of my patience, I also will *keep thee from the hour of temptation*, which shall come upon all the world, to try them that dwell upon the earth."**

There are several key words I want you to notice in this verse. First is the word *from*. The meaning of the Greek word used here is "out from."

Another key word is *hour*. This is not the Greek word for "sixty minutes," but for "an extended period of time." The Greek word for sixty minutes indicates a glance, a fleeting moment, but the Greek word used in verse 10 clearly indicates a longer period of time. Since Jesus is not referring to a literal hour, we understand that He is speaking about "the temptation that shall come upon the whole world to try them"—that is, the Tribulation. The Church is to be "kept out from" that "period of temptation."

Another key word is *temptation*. The Greek word actually means "trial" or "proof." The Church will not need proving because it will already have become the glorious church of Ephesians 5:27.

In Ephesians 4:11, God has set in the Church apostles, prophets, evangelists, pastors, and teachers for its perfection or spiritual growth. Ephesians Chapter 5, reveals Jesus presenting unto Himself a glorious Church without spot, wrinkle, or blemish. The Church being glorious at the time Jesus presents it to Himself indicates clearly that the ministry of apostles, prophets, evangelists, pastors, and teachers has been accepted. Therefore, the Church will be mature, united, and even increasing.

The Church will not need to be proven and tried by the Tribulation. It is being proven and tried now, and God's Word bear this out. *The church is going to be "kept out from" that period of trial because there is no need for the Church to experience it.* Furthermore, the Church will have become so glorious, the Father requests its presence in Heaven.

Jesus' Appearing Foretold in Prophecy

The Scripture concerning the appearing of Jesus and the results covers two full chapters of Revelation. The twenty-four elders and those whom they represent are the most important groups described in these two chapters.

Chapters 4 and 5 refer to the twenty-four elders who sit on thrones around God's throne. The number twenty-four immediately tells us they are representatives. The number twenty-four is the double of twelve: twelve representing the Old Testament saints and twelve representing the New Testament saints (See also Rev. 21:12-14.). The word *elder* in the Bible always identifies "one who has been set in the company of God's children for their leadership and exhortation. We know there will be more than twenty-four saints in heaven—there will be a vast company of God's children. So these twenty-four elders are literal representatives of that vast company.

John sees this company around God's throne before the Tribulation Period begins. Since these twenty-four are representatives, then whom do they represent? John described them as "the crystal sea"(Rev. 4:6). In Revelation 15:2, this sea is mingled with fire; the Holy Spirit (fire) is responsible for this huge company of righteous in Heaven.

The description of these elders confirms what is already taught. They are said to have crowns of gold, wear white robes, sit on thrones, and are associated with the prayers of the saints. They sing a new song of redemption, which the angels cannot sing. In that song they are clearly identified as being from all nations and peoples. They are earthlings, declaring they have been redeemed by the blood of the Lamb and they are kings and priests and will reign with Christ on earth. The redeemed saints of God have been victorious through Jesus Christ over everything that Satan has produced or tried to accomplish.

What a description! John sees them, not on earth, but before the throne! They are there before the first seal of Revelation 6 is opened to begin the Tribulation Period. As you can see, the Church must arrive in heaven or there will never be a "Tribulation Period" on earth.

God's Dealings with Israel

Daniel 9:24-27 establishes the period of time Jesus calls the Tribulation. Daniel clearly defines the Tribulation as a distinct seven-year period of time beginning with the Antichrist, the son of perdition. This man of sin comes on the scene and enters into an agreement with Israel. It is clearly stated that he does this at the beginning of the week. Daniel 9:24-27 reveals the seventy weeks of God's "determined dealings" with Israel. This is a prophecy which must be fulfilled. Some Bible teachers do not believe what is happening to the present nation of Israel is a fulfillment of God's Word, but I want you to know that it is. Many Old

Testament prophecies pertaining to Israel's restoration are now in the process of fulfillment.

Many Christians are ignorant concerning the importance of the nation of Israel. They are unaware that God has anything else to accomplish on the part of Israel. The subject is avoided by contending that Christians are the Israel of today and that there is no other. However, a study of Romans 11 proves otherwise. In Romans Chapter 11, Paul warns Christians not to confuse themselves with the natural seed of Abraham. The Church can be identified as the spiritual seed of Abraham, but there is also a natural seed, Israel, with which God has not yet finished His determined plans. *He must finish His work or His Word will fail.*

We are literally observing God restoring the nation of Israel; setting the stage to complete His final seven years of determined work and thus fulfill the prophecies of the Book of Daniel. Since all the previous sixty-nine weeks of Daniel's prophecies were seven years each, we know the last week will last seven years also. We are not allowed to shorten or lengthen the span of time set in Daniel 9:24-27.

In this same reference, we find that the man of sin who becomes the Antichrist at the beginning of that seven-year period, enters into an agreement with the nation of Israel.

Where will the Church be at that time? We have determined that the Lord will have already appeared to receive the glorious Church unto Himself.

The Church—the Restraining Factor

Daniel 9 is important, for it establishes exactly when the man of sin begins his activity. This man of sin who is to enter into an agreement with Israel cannot do so as long as the Church is here. 2 Thessalonians 2:1-9 makes it clear that the Antichrist, the man of sin, cannot be revealed until that which hinders or withholds him is gone. The Antichrist is the personification of the spirit of iniquity which was evident in Paul's day. That spirit of iniquity is lawlessness. We have no restraint for lawlessness on the earth today, except for the Holy Spirit-empowered Church.

There once was a time when lawlessness could be controlled by reminding a man of his moral responsibility. As recently as the 1930s and '40s, a man's word was his bond. Then as moral law and responsibility broke down, we turned to judicial law. We depended on legal documents and procedures to protect us. Now, even judicial law and order are oftentimes circumvented by ridiculous law suits.

The only true restraining factor for sin, godlessness, and lawlessness is the work of the Holy Spirit through the Church. Isaiah 59:19 says, **"When the enemy shall come in like a flood, the Spirit of the Lord shall lift up a standard against him."**

It is the specific assignment of the Holy Spirit to develop and work through the Church. Once He finishes that assignment (and He *will* finish it), His earthly assignment will then be to concentrate on the seven years of God's dealing with Israel.

The Word tells us that when the Holy Spirit has the Church at the peak of its maturity, it will be glorious enough to be received by Jesus. When the Holy Spirit-empowered Church is taken out of the way, the man of sin (the Antichrist) will be revealed. The removal of the Church will inaugurate the Tribulation Period for those who are left behind.

Comparing Daniel 9:24-27 with 2 Thessalonians 2:1-9, we can see that the Antichrist cannot begin his operation as long as the Church is on earth. Since Daniel reveals the Antichrist at the beginning of that seven-year period, we must conclude that the Church has been taken out of the way into heaven.

In 1 Thessalonians Chapter 4, we read Paul's description of the appearing of Jesus and our being caught up to meet Him in the air. In 2 Thessalonians Chapter II, he admonished the Thessalonian church to stand fast and not be shaken by those who were teaching that the "day of the Lord" had already come. He reminded them that this could not happen until "first there come a falling away" and "the man of sin" be revealed.

In verse 8, Paul tells us the Breath of the Lord's mouth—His Word—and the brightness of His coming will destroy the man of sin:

Even him, whose coming is after the working of Satan with all power and signs and lying wonders, and with all deceiveableness of unrighteousness in them that perish; because they received not the love of the truth, that they might be saved.
2 Thessalonians 2:9-10

Two Separate Events

In these verses, Paul writes about two different events involving the Lord Jesus Christ: in verse one, His appearing and our being gathered together unto Him; and in verse 8, His return to earth, at which time He destroys the Antichrist.

Paul was correcting the saints in Thessalonica because certain people had come with erroneous teachings and confused them. The same thing is going on today. Some sincere men are teaching erroneous things, traditions that are biblically unsound.

With just a little help from the Holy Spirit, it is not hard to understand this passage of Scripture. Both events—Christ's appearing to rapture His Church and His later return to establish His kingdom—are written about by the Apostle Paul. The two are separate and must not be confused. Paul makes it clear that the man of sin cannot be revealed and released to begin his reign during the Tribulation until the Church has been raptured by the Lord. Then, after the seven years of Tribulation, Christ will return to earth to establish His earthly kingdom. The first act of that reign will be to cast the Antichrist who opposed God and set himself up as God and his cohort, the False Prophet, alive into the Lake of Fire!

Methods, vehicles, and nations to be used by the Antichrist are being prepared right now, but the man of sin is not yet revealed. He is still being withheld and will be as long as we (the Church) are here and the Holy Spirit is at work in the Church. But once we have been taken up to meet the Lord in the air, the man of sin will be revealed (2 Thess. 2:7-8).

Revelation 6 reveals that when the Lord Jesus Christ opens the first seal, He is standing before God's throne. He is not sitting on the throne but standing before it with His company, as described in Revelation 4 and 5. He had left the throne in heaven descended and received His company, the righteous, unto Himself. He returns and walks to the throne, where He takes a book from His Father's hand, and makes ready to open the first seal.

The first seal produces a great deceiver, a man riding a white horse, using a bow but having no arrows. He is sent forth conquering and to conquer. He has no crown, so one is given to him. That certainly could not be Jesus. Jesus has many crowns. And He never uses a bow, only a two-edged sword. He does not go forth to conquer, because He has already overcome and conquered everything (John 16:33; Matt. 28:18).

The man who begins his activity at this time is none other than the Antichrist. His release heralds the beginning of the seven-year Tribulation Period on earth.

The "Next Resurrection" will also signal the onset of the seven-year period immediately preceding the one thousand-year reign of Christ. Known as the Tribulation, the Bible identifies this seven-year time frame as "the hour of trial which shall come upon the whole world, to test those who dwell on the earth" (Rev. 3:10 NKJV). Many have taught, and both books and movies have portrayed this as the time when the forces of evil become preeminent and dominate the world.

To the contrary, it will in fact be the hour of God's total victory over evil, as the massive harvest of souls that culminated with the rapture of the Church continues to increase right up until the very moment Jesus Himself returns with all His saints to rule and reign.

Now let's take a step into the future, beyond the next resurrection, to witness God's majestic handiwork as He inaugurates a special group of unmarried Jewish men to sweep this planet with the Good News for the next three and one-half years. The next phase of God's total victory over death is about to get underway.

---

[1] The Church is the army of Revelation 19:14, based on a number of Scriptures (2 Cor. 10:4; Eph. 6:10-18; 2 Tim. 2:1-4; Rev. 2:26,27).

[2] Why 24 elders representing the righteous? Twelve to represent the righteous of the tribes of Israel and 12 to represent the New Testament saints. The New Jerusalem described in Revelation 21 includes both companies (See vv. 12,14.).

[3] 2 Peter 2:12-13. Spots and blemishes.

[4] Spots, blemishes, and such are clearly defined and described in 2 Peter 2:9-19.

[5] Examine the prayer of Jesus recorded in John 17. You can be sure God will answer that prayer.

[6] Jeremiah 24 establishes the "fig tree" as a biblical type of Israel.

FIVE

THE GREAT MULTITUDE: THE FIFTH RAPTURE

Immediately after the "Next Resurrection" and the Rapture of the Church, God will select 144,000 Jewish evangelists to continue the preaching of the Gospel to the whole earth. They are sealed by God for their divine mission in Revelation 7:1-8 (NKJV).

> **After these things I saw four angels standing at the four corners of the earth, holding the four winds of the earth, that the wind should not blow on the earth, on the sea, or on any tree. Then I saw another angel ascending from the east, having the seal of the living God. And he cried with a loud voice to the four angels to whom it was granted to harm the earth and the sea, saying, "Do not harm the earth, the sea, or the trees till we have sealed the servants of our God on their foreheads." And I heard the number of those who were sealed. One hundred and forty-four thousand of all the tribes of the children of Israel were sealed:**

The fruit of their ministry will be the Great Multitude, who, like the Church three and one-half years earlier, when they are raptured at mid-Tribulation, will represent every one of the over six thousand language groups on earth.

The fifth rapture is the gathering together unto the Lord, or the catching up from earth to heaven, of these mid-Tribulation saints. It is recorded in Revelation 7, verses 9-17:

> **After this I beheld, and, lo, a great multitude, which no man could number, of all nations, and kindreds, and people, and tongues, stood before the throne, and before the Lamb, clothed with white robes, and palms in their hands; and cried with a loud voice, saying, Salvation to our God which sitteth upon the throne, and unto the Lamb.**
>
> **And all the angels stood round about the throne, and about the elders and the four beasts, and fell before the throne on their faces, and worshipped God, saying, Amen: Blessing, and glory, and wisdom, and thanksgiving, and honour, and power, and might, be unto our God for ever and ever, Amen.**
>
> **And one of the leaders answered, saying unto me, What are these which are arrayed in white robes? And whence came they?**
>
> **And I said unto him, Sir, thou knowest. And he said to me, These are they which came out of great tribulation, and have washed their robes, and made them white in the blood of the Lamb.**
>
> **Therefore are they before the throne of God, and serve him day and night in his temple: and he that sitteth on the throne shall dwell among them.**
>
> **They shall hunger no more, neither thirst any more; neither shall the sun light on them, nor any heat. For the Lamb which is in the midst of the throne shall feed them, and shall lead them unto living fountains of waters: and God shall wipe away all tears from their eyes.**

From this reference, we learn a fact that many do not know: a great number of people, probably about one billion, will be saved during the first three and one-half years of the Tribulation Period (a time I call "God's Master Performance"). Nowhere in the Scriptures is this exact figure given; it is a purely hypothetical estimate arrived at by computation based on the following end-time prophecy of Zechariah:

> **Thus saith the Lord of hosts; In those days** (the Tribulation Period) **it shall come to pass, that *ten men shall take hold* out of all languages of the nations, even shall take hold of the skirt *of him that is a Jew*, saying, We will go with you: for we have heard that God is with you.**
>
> Zechariah 8:23

If there are 15 million Jews on earth during the Tribulation, and ten Gentile men from every nation (plus women and children) are saved for every Jewish man, the total number saved could exceed one billion. The Bible says there will be a **"great multitude, which no man could number, of all nations, and kindreds, and people, and tongues."** These are the ones who will stand before the throne of God, **"clothed with white robes, and palms in their hands."**

This company (as tradition would have it) is not the Church of Jesus Christ. Rapture Number Four will take place *before* the Tribulation. This multitude will be saved during the first half of the Tribulation through the ministry of the 144,000 unmarried Jewish evangelists (Rev. 7 and 14).

Mid-Tribulation Saints

There is no question but that a great multitude is caught up at the midpoint of the Tribulation. When the Antichrist breaks his agreement with Israel, becoming hostile to them, he intends to destroy the Jews and Gentiles that were saved in the first half of the Tribulation. God intervenes by snatching them away to

Heaven. (It is very difficult to make war against someone who is no longer around!) God frustrates the devil's plan by simple taking these saints out of the way. Rapture Number Five.

When we carefully look at the description of those who are involved in this fifth rapture, we see clearly that they are not the redeemed Church of Jesus Christ. These people do not fit the description of the Body of Christ given in 1 Thessalonians 4 or Revelation 4 and 5.

When the Great Multitude is caught up to heaven there is no biblical record of the event being exactly like that of the catching away of the righteous, three and a half years earlier. They are not presented with crowns of gold; they do not sit on thrones; they do not sing the new song (they sing the song of Moses and the Lamb). It is strictly said of them: **"These are they which *came out of great tribulation,* and have washed their robes, and made them white in the blood of the Lamb"** (Rev. 7:14).

This verse suggests that these people already had robes of righteousness which they had soiled. (Otherwise, why would they need to cleanse them?) This is not the righteous Church company. These are the Tribulation saints—Israelis, backslidden Christians and prodigals—the multitudes who had some encounters with God and had been unfaithful servants. All such "foolish virgins" and lukewarm Christians who had not been looking for the return of our Lord can be put into this category (See Matt. 25:1-10 and Rev. 3:14-19.). Their robes, which were soiled, had to be cleansed in the blood of the Lamb. God is merciful.

But this is not a description of the Church and Old Testament saints. The saints of the Church Age are clearly described in Ephesians 5:27. Revelation 4 and 5 describes all the righteous together. They have crowns of gold; they sit upon thrones; they wear white robes; and they sing the new song, confessing to Jesus.

Thou art worthy . . . for thou wast slain, and hast redeemed us to God by thy blood out of every kindred, and tongue, and people, and nation; and hast made us unto our God kings and priests: and we shall reign on the earth.

Revelation 5:9-10

SIX

THE 144,000: THE SIXTH RAPTURE

Rapture Number Six is the rapture of the 144,000 Jewish evangelists, who are described in Revelation, chapters 7 and 14:

> And after these things I saw four angels standing on the four corners of the earth, holding the four winds of the earth, that the wind should not blow on the earth, nor on the sea, nor on any tree.
>
> And I saw another angel ascending from the east, having the seal of the living God: and he cried with a loud voice to the four angels, to whom it was given to hurt the earth and the sea, saying, Hurt not the earth, neither the sea, nor the trees, till we have sealed the servants of our God in their foreheads.
>
> And I heard the number of them which were sealed: and there were sealed *an hundred and forty and four thousand* of all the tribes of the children of Israel.
>
> Revelation 7:1-4

> And I looked, and lo, a Lamb stood on the mount Sion, and with him *an hundred forty and four thousand*, having his Father's name written in their foreheads.
>
> And I heard a voice from heaven, as the voice of many waters, and as the voice of a great thunder: and I heard the voice of harpers harping with their harps: and they sung as it were a new song before the

throne, and before the four beasts, and the elders: and no man could learn that song but *the hundred and forty and four thousand,* which were redeemed from the earth.

These are they which were not defiled with women; for they are virgins. These are they which follow the Lamb withersoever he goeth. These were redeemed from among men, being the first fruits unto God and to the Lamb.

And in their mouth was found no guile: for they are without fault before the throne of God.
(Note that verse 5 places the 144,000 before the throne of God—no longer on the earth.)

Revelation 14:1-5

These passages clearly describe the rapture of the 144,000 Jewish evangelists when they have finished their ministry. The primary ministry of these 144,000 was to the people of Israel. During the seven-year period of the Tribulation, God ministers directly to Israel through the 144,000 chosen Jewish evangelists.

Ministry to Israel

During these seven years, God deals not only with the Jewish nation of Israel but also Gentiles from all nations, tribes, and languages will be saved. As it is now, the ministry of God to all mankind is through the Church. But once the Church is taken up, God will return to completing His ministry to Israel. He will have only seven years in which to complete it.[1] During that time, the Gentiles who are saved will have to come in through the method God will use to bring all of Israel back to Himself: the ministry of the 144,000 thousand in the first three and a half years, and the ministry of angels in the second three and a half years.

This is how simple it is. Today, Jews are not excluded from coming into the Church. But when God has finished His direct work with the Gentiles, He will have to complete the last seven years of His determined work in behalf of Israel. This is described in Daniel 9:24-27. An important key to understanding Daniel's prophetic time frame is to know that Daniel's days are years. His seventy weeks are weeks of years, not days. Were they days, there would not be sufficient time for the events of his prophecy to come to pass. Convert his days to years, and one has a right amount of time for his events to come to pass.

God must finish His work in behalf of Israel. However, as the Prophet Zechariah revealed, during the first half of this seven-year period, ten times as many Gentile men (not counting women and children) as Jews will come into the Kingdom. These converts make up the great multitude (the fifth rapture) who stand before God's throne, as described in Revelation chapter 7.

When the 144,000 have finished their ministry to both Israel and many Gentiles, Jesus joins them at Mount Zion (Rev. 14:1). They learn the new song which the Church has been singing. This is the only other group, permitted to learn the new song (Rev. 14:3).

This reference tells us the approximate time they reach heaven. They arrive in time to learn the new song and join the Church at the wedding ceremony of the Lamb, which occurs somewhere during the second half of the seven-year Tribulation Period (Rev. 19). The ministry of the 144,000 lasts for approximately four to five of those seven years.

With the taking up of the 144,000, we have Rapture Number Six. There is a difference in the raptures we have discussed. The first three involved individuals—Enoch, Elijah, and Jesus. Raptures Four, Five, and Six will involve great multitudes of people. It is just as easy for God to take up a great multitude as to rapture an individual. Quantity is no problem for God.

---

[1] A study of Daniel 9:24-27 reveals God's period of 490 years (70 weeks, with each lasting 7 years), in which He is determined to accomplish the six things listed in verse 24. There are fixed events in this passage, clearly establishing a remainder of 7 years.

SEVEN

THE TWO WITNESSES: THE SEVENTH RAPTURE

Rapture Number Seven is the rapture of the two witnesses, found in Revelation 11:3-12:

> And I will give power unto *my two witnesses*, and they shall prophesy a thousand two hundred and threescore days, clothed in sackcloth.
>
> These are the two olive trees, and the two candlesticks standing before the God of the earth.
>
> And if any man will hurt them, fire proceedeth out of their mouth, and devoureth their enemies: and if any man will hurt them, he must in this manner be killed.
>
> These have power to shut heaven, that it rain not in the days of their prophecy: and have power over waters to turn them to blood, and to smite the earth with all plagues, as often as they will.
>
> And when they shall have finished their testimony, the beast that ascendeth out of the bottomless pit shall make war against them, and shall overcome them, and kill them. And their dead bodies shall lie in the street of the great city, which spiritually is called Sodom and Egypt, where also our Lord was crucified.
>
> And they of the people and kindreds and tongues and nations shall see their dead bodies three

THE TWO WITNESSES: THE SEVENTH RAPTURE

days and an half, and shall not suffer their dead bodies to be put in graves.

And they that dwell upon the earth shall
rejoice over them, and make merry, and shall send
gifts one to another; because these two prophets tor-
mented them that dwelt on the earth.

And after three days and an half the Spirit of
life from God entered into them, and they stood upon
their feet; and great fear fell upon them which saw
them. And they heard a great voice from heaven saying unto them, Come up hither.

And they *ascended up to heaven in a cloud;*
and their enemies beheld them.

Once the Antichrist has broken his agreement with Israel,
he invades that nation and sets up headquarters in a temple at
Jerusalem. Immediately, two men appear in the street before his
headquarters and begin a countdown of judgment against the
Antichrist. Unsuccessfully, the Antichrist tries to destroy them.
Only four days before the end of that seven-year period, he again
sends his security forces against these two men. This time God
allows them to be killed.

The World Watches

For three and one-half days, their dead bodies lie in the
street, while the crowds who follow the Antichrist celebrate by
exchanging gifts and making merry, saying, "those two who tor-
mented us are dead and we are glad!" The entire world views the
scene as it is undoubtedly broadcast on television via satellite.

After those three and one-half days, with the television
cameras still operating, life from God reenters those dead bodies
and they are resurrected, while the whole world watches! The two
witnesses are raptured as God's voice is heard from heaven:
"Come up here!" The two witnesses then ascend, just as those

78

before them—Enoch, Elijah, Jesus, the Church, the 144,000 Jewish evangelists, and the Tribulation saints.

Imagine how shocked the TV cameramen will be as they start panning the ascension, following the two witnesses up, up, all the way to heaven! As the skies roll back like a scroll, the world looks right into the face of God! (See Rev. 6:12-17.)

Then there occurs an upheaval of nature like the world has never known. Jesus comes charging back to earth, with all His angels and the saints who had been caught up to heaven. Back to earth they come! What an event to behold!

Eight

Jesus' Return

We have carefully examined the appearing of Jesus, which is the first of two events that make up His Second Coming. The second of these is His return to earth. It is altogether different from His appearing.

So Christ was once offered to bear the sins of many; and unto them that look for him shall he appear the second time without sin unto salvation.

Hebrews 9:28

Here we learn two things—we are to look for His appearing and, at His appearing, He will have absolutely nothing to do with sin. When He came the first time, He had to become sin (a sin offering), so that we who believe might be set free from sin. He became sin (a sin offering), so that He might pay the total ransom price for those who would believe in Him.He was the great substitutionary sacrifice offered once and for all for our sins (2 Cor. 5:21).

At His appearing, He will perform the final act of salvation, which is the glorification of our bodies. Today our spirits and souls are enjoying full salvation, but our bodies are not. Full salvation for our bodies means they become glorified and immortal.

When Jesus returns to Earth to reign, He must again handle sin, not the way He handled it the first time, but by destroying the followers of Satan, those who are destroying the earth (Rev. 11:18).

The Battle of Armageddon

Now let's read from the writings of Zechariah, an Old Testament prophet:

> **Behold, the day of the Lord cometh** (the day He returns to establish His Kingdom), **and thy spoil shall be divided in the midst of thee. For I will gather all nations against Jerusalem to battle** (the Battle of Armageddon); **and the city shall be taken, and the houses rifled, and the women ravished; and half of the city shall go forth into captivity, and the residue of the people shall not be cut off from the city.**
>
> **Then shall the Lord go forth, and fight against those nations, as when he fought in the day of battle.** (You can see that the Lord gets involved in the Battle of Armageddon.)
>
> **And his feet shall stand in that day upon the mount of Olives, which is before Jerusalem on the east, and the mount of Olives shall cleave in the midst thereof toward the east and toward the west, and there shall be a very great valley; and half of the mountain shall remove toward the north, and half of it toward the south.**
>
> **And ye shall flee to the valley of the mountains; for the valley of the mountains shall each unto Azal: yea, ye shall flee, like as ye fled from before the earthquake in the days of Uzziah king of Judah: and the Lord my God shall come, and <u>all</u> the saints with thee.**
>
> **Zechariah 14:1-5**

All the righteous saints had to be in heaven with Jesus or they could not be returning to earth with Him. When the Lord returns from heaven to stand upon the Mount of Olives for the Battle of Armageddon, all the saints will return with Him. This is a thrilling and exciting revelation of truth. This event harmonizes with the seventh angelic trumpet of Revelation 11:15-19.

Changes in Light

In Zechariah 14:6 the Battle of Armageddon begins: **"And it shall come to pass in that day, that the light shall not be clear, nor dark."**

During a brief period of time, there will be no natural light from the sun, moon, or stars. According to Revelation 16:10, natural light will be withheld form "the seat of the beast," identifying the geographical area over which the Antichrist has gained control. Some think he will control the whole world, but he never does. He would like to, but God interferes. In fact, Revelation 6:8 reveals the antichrist will only control one-fourth of the earth.

The area of the world controlled by the Antichrist (the Middle East, the Mediterranean, and Europe, in particular) will be totally dark for a number of days. On this last day of Tribulation —the day Jesus is to return—there will be some light, but it will not increase. The sky will remain a sort of eerie gray. **"But it shall be one day which shall be know to the Lord, not day, nor night: but it shall come to pass, that at evening time it shall be light" (Zech. 14:7).**

Why would it be light at a time when it ordinarily would be getting dark? Because the Battle of Armageddon will then be over. Those who have been destroying the earth will have been destroyed. The Antichrist and False Prophet will have been cast into the lake of fire. Satan will have been bound and cast into the bottomless pit for a thousand years. Jesus will have taken over the governments of the world and begun His thousand-year reign. It will be so glorious that at evening the sun will be bright!

> And it shall be in that day, that living waters shall go out from Jerusalem; half of them toward the former sea, and half of them toward the hinder sea: in summer and in winter shall it be.
>
> Zechariah 14:8

The great earthquake that divides the Mount of Olives will make a port out of the city of Jerusalem. Waters will flow from one sea to the other—the Mediterranean to the Dead Sea.

> And the Lord shall be king over all the earth: in that day shall there be one Lord, and his name one.
>
> All the land shall be turned as a plain from Geba to Rimmon south of Jerusalem: and it shall be lifted up, and inhabited in her place, from Benjamin's gate unto the place of the first gate, unto the corner gate, and from the tower of Hananeel unto the king's winepresses.
>
> And men shall dwell in it, and there shall be no more utter destruction; but Jerusalem shall be safely inhabited.
>
> And this shall be the plague wherewith the Lord will smite all the people that have fought against Jerusalem.
>
> Zechariah 14:9-12

All the armies[1] Satan could gather to come against Jerusalem for the Battle of Armageddon have been gathered in the valley of Megiddo, stretching into the plains of Jezreel. The Lord returns and stands on the Mount of Olives. He speaks the Word and it goes forth out of His mouth like a two-edged sword to destroy the armies of the Antichrist and the kings of the east at the Battle of Armageddon:

> Their flesh shall consume away while they stand upon their feet, and their eyes shall consume

away in their holes, and their tongue shall consume away in their mouth.

And it shall come to pass in that day, that a great tumult from the Lord shall be among them; and they shall lay hold every one on the hand of his neighbour, and his hand shall rise up against the hand of his neighbour. And Judah also shall fight at Jerusalem; and the wealth of all the heathen round about shall be gathered together, gold, and silver, and apparel, in great abundance.

And so shall be the plague of the horse, of the mule, of the camel, and of the ass, and of all the beasts that shall be in these tents, as this plague.

Zechariah 14:12-15

Jesus speaks the Word from the Mount of Olives which releases the plague to smite the vast Oriental armies and the armies of the Antichrist (Zech. 14:12). They are immediately blinded; their eyes consumed away in their sockets. They are immediately dumb; their tongues consumed away in their mouths. In fright, they reach out and grab one another for security. That only frightens them more, so they turn to fight among themselves. Their flesh begins to fall away from their bones. Their blood gushes to the earth, creating the pool of blood described in Revelation 14: 17-20. It stretches over an area of about two hundred square miles in the valley of Megiddo.

In Zechariah 14, we see the events that take place at the Lord's return to earth. You can readily see the distinct difference between His return and His appearing.

Now let's look at Revelation, chapters 19 and 20. I want you to be well established in the authority of God's Word so that you will not be shaken by doctrines of error.

In Revelation 19:11, we pick up the final day of the Tribulation and the return of Christ to earth: **"And I saw heaven opened, and behold a white horse; and he that sat upon him was called Faithful and True, and in righteousness he doth judge and make war."**

We are able to identify the rider of this white horse. (The rider in Rev. 6:2 cannot be personally identified because that rider is the Antichrist.) This rider is called Faithful and True. He is our Lord Jesus Christ! What does He do? **"In righteousness he doth judge and make war."**

A God of Wrath

Many people believe that our God has nothing to do with war. Others see Him only as a God of love. They think they can live any way they like and God will do nothing. Those people need to read the entire Book. There is more to the nature of God than just love. He is a God of anger, wrath, and furious indignation. He is a God Who will not acquit the wicked. He *is* love, and we are permitted to meet Him in His love rather than in His wrath. However, we need to discover the love of God and all the aspects of His divine nature.

John continues with His description in Revelation 19:12-13 & 15:

> **His eyes were as a flame of fire, and on his head were many crowns; and he had a name written, that no man knew, but he himself.**
> **And he was clothed with a vesture dipped in blood: and his name is called the Word of God.**
> **And out of his mouth goeth a sharp sword, that with it he should smite the nations: and he shall rule them with a rod of iron: and he treadeth the winepress of the fierceness and wrath of Almighty God.**

The closing verses of Revelation 19 are a preview of the Battle of Armageddon and the winepress that creates a pool of blood in the valley of Megiddo. Jesus is the one who treads the winepress. Standing on the Mount of Olives, He speaks the Word of God that releases the plague of Zechariah 14:12 to destroy the armies gathered for the Battle of Armageddon.

> **And he hath on his vesture and on his thigh a name written, KING OF KINGS, AND LORD OF LORDS.**
>
> **And I saw an angel standing in the sun; and he cried with a loud voice, saying to all the fowls that fly in the midst of heaven, Come and gather yourselves together unto the supper of the great God; that ye may eat the flesh of kings, and the flesh of captains, and the flesh of mighty men, and the flesh of horses, and of them that sit on them, and the flesh of all men, both free and bond, both small and great.**
>
> **And I saw the beast, and the kings of the earth, and their armies, gathered together to make war against him that sat on the horse, and against his army.**
>
> **And the beast was taken, and with him the false prophet that wrought miracles before him, with which he deceived them that had received the mark of the beast, and them that worshipped his image. These both were cast alive into a lake of fire burning with brimstone.**
>
> **And the remnant were slain with the sword of him that sat upon the horse, which sword proceeded out of his mouth: and all the fowls were filled with their flesh.**
>
> **Revelation 19:16-21**

Satan and Sin Defeated!

The opening verses of Revelation 20:1-4 reads:

> **And I saw an angel come down from heaven, having the key of the bottomless pit and a great chain in his hand.**
>
> **And he laid hold on the dragon, that old serpent, which is the Devil, and Satan, and bound him a thousand years,**
>
> **And cast him into the bottomless pit, and shut him up, and set a seal upon him, that he should deceive the nations no more, till the thousand years should be fulfilled: and after that he must be loosed a little season.**
>
> **And I saw thrones, and they sat upon them, and judgment was given unto them: and I saw the souls of them that were beheaded for the witness of Jesus, and for the word of God, and which had not worshipped the beast, neither his image, neither had received his mark upon their foreheads, or in their hands; and they lived and reigned with Christ a thousand years.**

You can readily see what happens at the return of Jesus. Satan is bound and cast into the bottomless pit for a thousand years. All the martyred saints of the Tribulation Period are resurrected and enter into a relationship with the Lord Jesus Christ and all the other saints (Rev. 20:4). These events coincide with the return of Christ to Earth.

There are distinct differences between the appearing of Christ and His return. The Church is caught up before the first day of the Tribulation Period. Then Christ returns to earth to reign on the last day of the Tribulation.

Look for Jesus! Be among those who are watching, praying, and looking for His appearing (Luke 21:36; Heb. 9:28). Join other Christians in the harvest fields laboring and enjoying the work of the Holy Spirit. Don't listen to erroneous teachings that strip away that blessed hope which is yours—the glorious appearing of our Lord and Savior Jesus Christ (Titus 2:13).

---

[1] The Antichrist will bring ten armies to the Battle of Armageddon (see Rev. 17:10-14). He will also have the support of the Orientals of Revelation 9:13-19 and 16:12 -16.

SUMMARY

The Second Coming involves two major events: the appearing of Jesus to receive the glorious Church, and the actual return of Jesus to reign for one thousand years on earth.

At His appearing, the mature and gloriously productive Church will be caught up with the resurrected saints to return with Jesus to Heaven. This clears the way for the revealing of the Antichrist and the beginning of the Tribulation.

Christ returns to earth seven years later with all of his saints. At that time, He will destroy the armies of the Antichrist at Armageddon. He causes the Antichrist and the False Prophet to be cast alive into the lake of fire. Then, as Satan is bound and cast into the bottomless pit for one thousand years, Jesus begins His reign of peace and righteousness, exercising authority over all the nations.

It is not difficult to understand the difference between these two events. Daniel points out in Chapter 9 exactly when the Antichrist will begin his activity, which is at the beginning of the seven-year Tribulation Period. How wonderful is Paul's statement in 2 Thessalonians 2:7-8 that the Church must be removed before the wicked one can be revealed.

With the Church taken out of the way and the release of the Antichrist occurring at the onset of the Tribulation, we can clearly see that the Church has absolutely no place on earth during the seven years of Tribulation.

The Church is not pictured on earth after chapter 5 of Revelation until it is described returning with Christ in chapter 19. God is not confused, neither does He make mistakes.

I pray that this book has helped you to understand the Second Coming of Jesus, which includes His glorious appearing to rapture His Church and His return to reign on earth. I pray that you now understand that both are part of the Second Coming of our Lord, but are two different events separated by seven years.

My prayer is that you are not only looking for His appearing, but are also reaching out to others so they, too, may become aware of the appearing of Jesus Christ which is soon to take place.

Thank You, Heavenly Father, for Your beautiful and simple Word. Thank You also for the Holy Spirit Who provides us with proper understanding. To You, Father, be all glory and power!

Evangelizing the World Through the Prophecies of the Scripture

Hilton Sutton is regarded by many as one of the world's foremost authorities on Bible prophecy as related to current events and world affairs. Celebrating fifty-two years of ministry this year, Dr. Hilton Sutton presents the prophecies of the scripture in an edifying manner, free from doom, gloom, and speculation. He dismisses commonly taught but unbiblical eschatological themes, such as an imminent economic collapse, a coming one-world government ruled by a world dictator, and a great falling away. Instead, he clearly demonstrates that the Bible foretells prosperity throughout the closing hours of this age, and the greatest harvest of souls ever by the glorious, victorious army of God, the Church; a harvest that, after the Rapture of the Church, will continue to grow throughout the seven years of Tribulation until we return with Jesus and all the saints to establish the first and only world government, the one thousand year reign of our Lord.

Other Books by Hilton Sutton Th.D

- *The Antichrist*
- *Discovering Ancient Prophecies*
- *Revelation Revealed*
- *The Revelation Teaching Syllabus*
- *Deacons*
- *The United States in Prophecy*

AUTHOR CONTACT

For more information regarding this ministry contact us at:

Hilton Sutton World Ministries
2434 Roman Forest Blvd
Roman Forest, TX 77357

Hilton Sutton World Ministries
P.O. Box 1259
New Caney, TX 77357

Phone: (281) 689-1260
Fax: (281) 689-1265
www.hilton-sutton.org

In Canada Contact:
Hilton Sutton World Ministries—Canada
104-4053 Meadowbrook Dr
London ON N6L 1E8

Phone: (519) 652-2232
vcc.bds@sympatico.ca